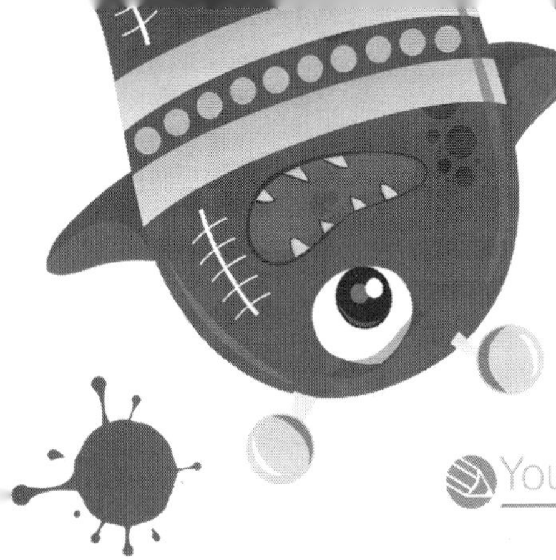

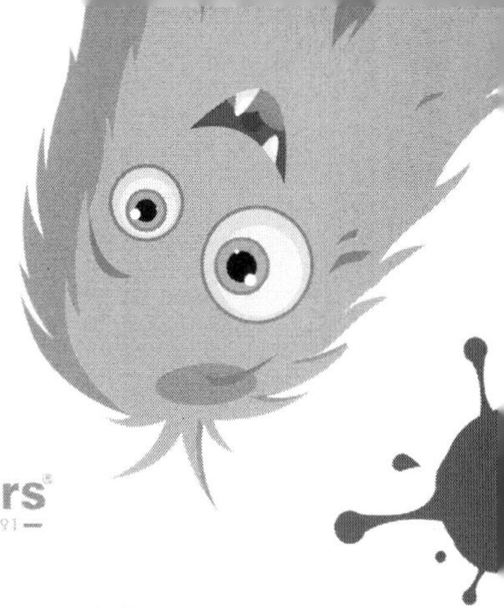

YoungWriters
Est. 1991

MONSTER POETRY

Creature Features

Edited By Sarah Waterhouse

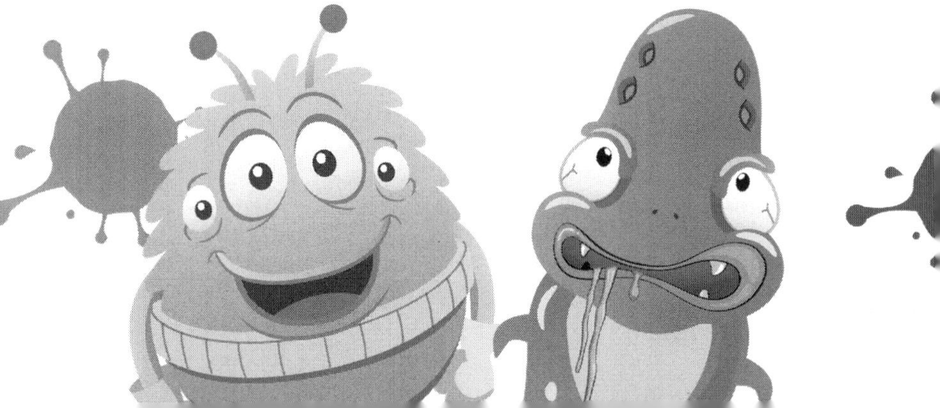

First published in Great Britain in 2023 by:

Young Writers
Remus House
Coltsfoot Drive
Peterborough
PE2 9BF
Telephone: 01733 890066
Website: www.youngwriters.co.uk

All Rights Reserved
Book Design by Ashley Janson
© Copyright Contributors 2023
Softback ISBN 978-1-80459-752-1

Printed and bound in the UK by BookPrintingUK
Website: www.bookprintinguk.com
YB0555I

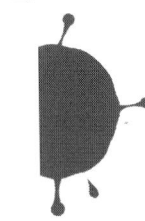

Foreword

Young Writers was created in 1991 with the express purpose of promoting and encouraging creative writing. Each competition we create is tailored to the relevant age group, giving each child the inspiration and incentive to create their own piece of writing, whether it's a poem or a short story. We truly believe that seeing it in print gives pupils a sense of achievement and pride in their work and themselves.

Our latest competition, Monster Poetry, focuses on uncovering the different techniques used in poetry and encouraging pupils to explore new ways to write a poem. Using a mix of imagination, expression and poetic styles, this anthology is an impressive snapshot of the inventive, original and skilful writing of young people today. These poems showcase the creativity and talent of these budding new writers as they learn the skills of writing, and we hope you are as entertained by them as we are.

Contents

All Saints C W Primary School, Llanedeyrn

Poppy Gibbons (10)	1
Tillie Lewis (11)	2
Owen Belcher (9)	4
Emily Rogerson (11)	5
Rosie Smith (10)	6

Bervie School, Montrose

Charlotte O'Donnell (10)	7
Michael Barnard (10)	8
Eilidh Murdoch (9)	10
Dennis Milne (9)	12
William Morris (9)	14
Vinnie Walker (9)	15
Rebecca Rae (10)	16
Ivy Tait (10)	17
Freya Wilson (9)	18
Emily Shaw (9)	19
Hannah Knights (9)	20
Danielle Bagnall (10)	21
Angus Jacobsen (9)	22
Jaxon Lawrie (10)	23
Mia Rae (9)	24
Ayana Van Rooyen (10)	25

Gorsey Bank Primary School, Wilmslow

Nellie Branagan (9)	26
Oliver Conoley (9)	28
Beatrice Mellor (8)	30
Charlotte Gay (8)	32
Till Knight (9)	34

Jake Woods (9)	35
Romy Cliff (9)	36
Albie Croston (8)	37
Sam Walton (8)	38
Holly Hosie (9)	39
William Goffredo (9)	40
Bobby McCamley (8)	41
Amelie Hargreaves (9)	42
Leo Munsch (9)	43
Madeleine Boardman (9)	44
Darcy Dick (9)	45
Jack Shuttleworth (9)	46
Henry Jones (9)	47
Arabella Durow (9)	48
Zarrah Sardar (9)	49
Rupert Burnham (9)	50
Elliott Cartwright (9)	51
Nigel Man (9)	52
Leo Wiltshire (9)	54
Jenson Higby (9)	55
Skyla George (9)	56
Clara Stockdill (9)	57
Alexandra Martin (8)	58
Lucas Wright (9)	59
Leo Ritchie (9)	60
Archie Jones (9)	61
Robyn Howard (9)	62
Olivia Mainwaring (9)	63
Frederick Hitch (9)	64
Jacob Beetson (9)	65
Zainuddin Ahmed (8)	66
Charlie Manton (9)	67
Poppy Favour (9)	68
Jude Wolstenholme (9)	69
Kaasim Khaliq (9)	70

Neve Atkinson (9)	71
Hugo Ashurst (9)	72
Thomas O'Shea (8)	73
Jemima Langman (9)	74
Theo Clarke (8)	75
Alfie Little (9)	76
Lucy Loughhead (9)	77
Sophie Sharman (9)	78
Aston Tyler (9)	79
James Aughton (9)	80
Benjamin Shaw (9)	81
Jamie Wong (8)	82
William Graham (9)	83
Tom Davies (8)	84
Hanoch Rino (8)	85
Olivia Bauer (9)	86

Hermitage Primary School, Helensburgh

Niamh Hackett (9)	87
Poppy Hall (8)	88
Georgia Dow (9)	89
Nyla Troup (8)	90
Ciaran McHardy (8)	91
Lewis Aitken (9)	92
Katie Buchanan (8)	93
Georgia Mccallion (9)	94
Charlotte Boyle (9)	95
Miller Hill (8)	96
Willow Muir (9)	97
John Edwardson (8)	98
Harlow McKenna (8)	99
Kyle Welsh (8)	100
James Wightwick (9)	101
Olivia-Jo Cameron (8)	102
Caris Reilly (8)	103

Kirknewton Primary School, Kirknewton

Penny Turner (9)	104
Grace McNee (8)	106
Lily Scallon (9)	107
Martha Bowman (9)	108
Esther Shaw (9)	109
Ethan Cook (8)	110
Myla D'Arcy (9)	111
Jack Watson (8)	112
Laura Blain (9)	113
Arwin Chawla (8)	114
Islay Mitchell (8)	115
Charlotte Jack (8)	116
Finlay Nicol (8)	117
Ailsa Goldie (8)	118
Ellen Clark (8)	119
Anabelle Jagla (9)	120
Emanuel Shiels (8)	121
Harris Blair (8)	122
Natalie Berry (9)	123
Emma Dicker (9)	124
Sophie Ward (9)	125

Ossett Holy Trinity CEVA Primary School, Ossett

Lydia Boome (8)	126
Katie Ibbetson (8)	128
Hollie Roberts (8)	129
Evelyne Croft (8)	130
Thomas Milnes (8)	131
Hettie Walters (7)	132
Alex Ciobanu (7)	133

Our Lady Of The Assumption Primary School, Belle Vale

Dexter Jones (8)	134
Owen Barnes (7)	135
Amelie Gorman (8)	136
Ava Gorman (8)	137
Alfie Viner (8)	138

South Norwood Primary School, South Norwood

Edwina Attim (9)   139

St Anne's And Guardian Angels Catholic Primary School, London

Eldana Liewi (9)	140
Flora Afolabi (9)	142
Reggie Matthews (9)	144
Isla Goodchild (8)	146
Zael Rose-Achiampong (9)	148
Ruby Ader-Wrightson (9)	149
Maisha Delannoy (8)	150
Eliana Tekel (9)	152
Stella Leiva Ospina (9)	153
Olivia Darby (8)	154

St Charles Borromeo Catholic Primary School, Weybridge

Luke Wong (8)	155
Breah Rough (8)	156
Chloe Greenrod (8)	159
Amelie Brown (8)	160
Luca Fumagalli (7)	162
Ruby Lee (8)	164
Kitty Macdougall (7)	166
Cassandra Pollicar (8)	167
Daisy Cooper (8)	168
Melissa Vacarro (8)	169
Colin Wong (8)	170
Sebastian Gibson (8)	171
Eli-James Frontado (8)	172
Alicia Barnea Choi (7)	173
Cian Wilson (8)	174
Peter Counsell (8)	175
Edmund Santamaria (8)	176
Christian Muzengi (7)	177
Jonas Baptista (7)	178
Oliver Wever (8)	179
Benjamin Wright (8)	180
William Sifton (8)	181

Avery Gibson (7)   182

Surlingham Community Primary School, Surlingham

Mannix Grant (9)	183
Freya Dunning (7)	184
Hugo McKinney (8)	186
Penny Gregory (9)	187
Oliver Lincoln (8)	188
Toby S (9)	189
Izaac Fisher (8)	190
Oran Grant (9)	191
Ella Hambling (8)	192
Lee Codling (8)	193
Sadie Rae (9)	194
Arthur Hall (8)	195

Ysgol Carreg Hirfaen, Cwmann

Libby Howell (7)	196
Tirion Tomos (11)	198
Emelia Howell (8)	200
Lilybet Cousinne (10)	202
Oleanna Cousinne (8)	203
Poppy Griffiths (11)	204
Jessica Burtenshaw-Jones (7)	205
Esther Jones (9)	206
Mair Hopkins (11)	207
Tom Hari (10)	208
Lisa Adcock Williams (8)	209
Jacob Hall (8)	210
Chloe Ling (10)	211
Benjamin Davies (7)	212
Ifan Jones (10)	213
Alis Jones (11)	214
Cerys Jones (11)	215
Llio Richards (11)	216
Callum Gale (8)	217
Elin Dafydd Lewis (11)	218
Menna Greasley (10)	219
Theo Syrett-Bibby (9)	220
Erica Burtenshaw-Jones (9)	221
Morgan Williams (8)	222

Name	Number
Ava-May Gregson (8)	223
Celyn Efa Jones (9)	224
Lili Jones (9)	225
Poppy Scaife (8)	226
Nia (8)	227
John Lewis (9)	228
Sebastian Jac Gregson (9)	229
Mia Hargreaves (11)	230
Amelia Edwards (11)	231
Megan Thomas (11)	232
Amelia Rees (8)	233
Cai Davies (10)	234
Brychan Richards (8)	235
Joshua Davies (10)	236
Henry Gillard (8)	237
Celt Davies (9)	238
Jake Jones (10)	239
Elin Hopkins (9)	240
Siwan Haf Davies (7)	241
Gwion Howden (7)	242
Cara Jones (9)	243
Tomos Evans (10)	244
Evie Haf Williams (8)	245
Ellis Jones (9)	246
Aron Russell (8)	247
Oliver Readwin (11)	248
Eva Bevan (8)	249
Rheinallt Davies (10)	250
Zoe Evans (8)	251
Leo Gale (8)	252
Evie Langford (7)	253
Gruff Pexton (7)	254
Niamh Jones (9)	255
Cadi Fflur Davies (10)	256
Cai Jones (8)	257
Cadi Rowcliffe (8)	258
Kyron Lloyd White (7)	259
Charlie Scaife (8)	260

The Poems

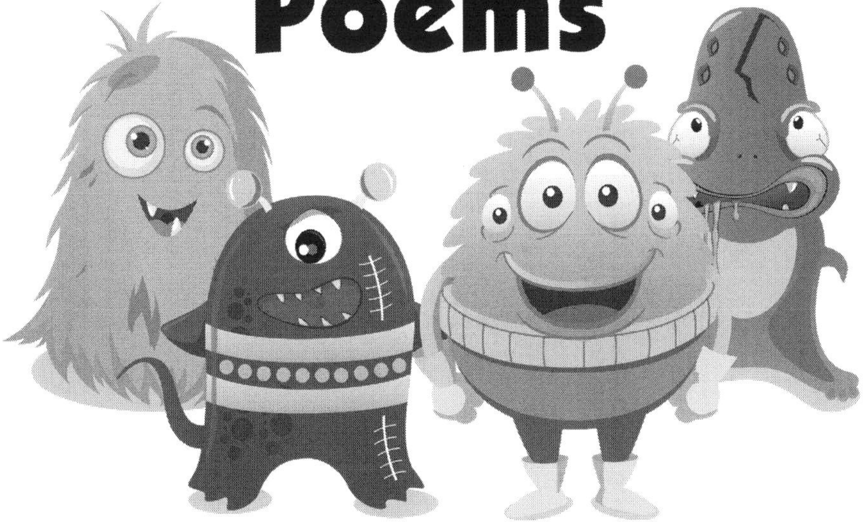

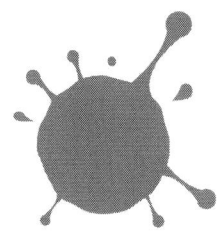
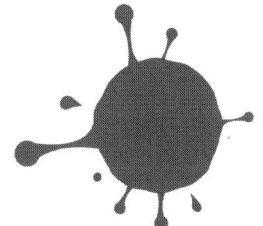

Monster Poetry - Creature Features

Mystery Under The Bed...

Have you ever had a feeling something's lurking below,
In the shadows, under the bed or behind the door?
Nobody knows.
Witness after witness, but still nobody believes,
He is stinky like toilet water, he's worse than
Our dreams.
Eyes he's got infinite, he's awake every second
Is it true, do you reckon?
With mushrooms on his head, that's where all his
Eyes are kept
Once he's done with you, you'll wish you
Never slept,
When you search and search, he turns invisible
Only his razor-sharp claws are visible,
At night, he sneaks out from under your bed,
He feeds you his potions, you magically grow,
That's why adults are tall, he's not done with you
at all.

Poppy Gibbons (10)
All Saints C W Primary School, Llanedeyrn

The Hairy Monster

T he first time you see the hairy monster, he might look a bit scary
H e is very smelly and looks a bit like jelly
E ven if you take him to the hairdressers, he will still look hairy

H e has fluffy fur, huge horns and enormous eyes
A ttractive: the hairy monster has never heard
I think the hairy monster is cute, others think he is the scariest monster there is
R ats are the hairy monster's favourite food, he gobbles them up for dinner
Y achts are the hairy monster's transport, far away in the sea where nobody can see him.

M y best friend is the hairy monster, we do everything together
O ld Hairy Monster (Grandpa Monster) has the longest hair in the world
N obody plays with me and Hairy Monster, we run, run, run around the park at night
S o many people think that monsters are not real
T ogether, me and Monster do lots of things together, we paint our nails, do crafts and play tag

E very day, when I go to school, I miss Hairy Monster.
R emember Hairy Monster because if you see him, remember is not scary!

Tillie Lewis (11)
All Saints C W Primary School, Llanedeyrn

Seedlox

In a forest deep, Seedlox creeps.
Slow and thin with his tail tucked in.
Creatures hide from his trembling cry.
A keen glint in the eye...
Seedlox leaps,
Arms out -
Like a frog,
And casually startles a bold black dog.
The dog whimpers with fright as Seedlox advances,
And fleeing with fear, it gusts into the branches.
Now Seedlox, alone, only wants to be trusted.
Yet, when creatures see him they're only disgusted.
Will any awaken and see his disguise
Is only a front,
And not his inside?

Owen Belcher (9)
All Saints C W Primary School, Llanedeyrn

The Cuddly Creature

C uddly, kind, shy - have you ever heard of a monster like this? No, you have not because my monster, Coco, is unique and diverse to all the other monsters.

O bviously I love her to bits, her nails are a bit sharp and grimy, but still I love her to bits!

C uddly, a bit whiffy at times... Do not try to brush her hair, it is like scrambled spaghetti... I love her even though she does have nits!

O kay, that does not matter... Despite the hair and the smell and the nits, Coco, the cuddly creature... I love her to bits!

Emily Rogerson (11)
All Saints C W Primary School, Llanedeyrn

The Gat

T he Gat is a square invisible monster
H ere
E ach day, he is very

G ood
A nd goes all around
T he soil.

Rosie Smith (10)
All Saints C W Primary School, Llanedeyrn

Monster Poetry - Creature Features

All Around The World

My name is Flower Devil.
I live in the basement of an abandoned school.
I am as strong as a silverback gorilla
Weight-lifting the heaviest metal in the world.
I came out of my lair to torture the town.
But before I could fully come out
I saw this yacht poster
To go all the way around the world.
The first place I stopped at was Russia
Then Italy, Ukraine, Mexico, Florida, to say hello to my cousins.
The last place I stopped at was Paris.
The biggest thing I wanted to do
Was destroy the Eiffel Tower
But when I got there
There was a dragon sleeping on it
I tried stabbing its body
What I didn't realise was that it was staring right at me
And tried to kill me.

Charlotte O'Donnell (10)
Bervie School, Montrose

Killar

One sunny afternoon, I went to the
Park after school.
My friends were there and they
Were acting the fool.
In the corner of the park was a
Monster looking sad,
So I brought him home with me,
Which was bad!

Monster was little and slimy,
He told me his name was Killar,
Oh blimey!
He was born in a lab, in Scotland
In June
One night, when there was a full
Moon.

The next day, I took the monster to school.
I knew, straight away, he would
Break every rule.
At break time, he told me he killed
Timmy before the bell.

I did notice the playground had a
Funny smell.
I was shocked, but I didn't tell on
Him.
But the smell was so grim.
So, the head teacher searched the school
Ground
And Timmy's body she found.
Her face went very pale.
And the police took Killar to jail.
Tomorrow, after school, I'll just play in
My den.

Michael Barnard (10)
Bervie School, Montrose

Liv And Dev's Adventure

My monster's name is Liv and Dev.
They are two monsters combined.
I met Liv and Dev at my school
They came to my class in P5 for a day
Dev is really naughty, but Liv is really nice
Liv and Dev are my new friends
Dev says she was found in a fire in London
Liv says she was found in a fluffy cloud also in London
They made friends with a monster
Called Hovering Holly
She is one of my friends too.
Dev is bullying everyone!
Except me and Hovering Holly of course
Liv is as good as gold.
They started to argue about what to do at lunch
But then they decided they were
Going to play with me and Hovering Holly
But Dev got called back into the classroom
To speak to the teacher about her behaviour
She was *not happy* with Dev

Sadly, Liv and Dev had to go
Liv went back to her fluffy cloud in London
Dev went back to her fire also in London.

Eilidh Murdoch (9)
Bervie School, Montrose

Bob, The Friendly Monster

Bob the Monster met me after school
We were going to my house, but my house was very far away.
When we were walking, we passed Cosmos and Bob wanted to go.
"Please, please can we go in? I have been a good monster."
"No," I said, "we need to go to my house," and kept walking.
Then we went past Codonas and Bob wanted to go.
"Please, please can we go? I have been a good monster."
"No," I said, we needed to go to my house and we kept walking.
Then we went past a clothes shop and Bob wanted to go.
"Please, please can we go? I have been a good monster."
"No," I said, "we need to go to my house," and we kept walking.

Then we went past my house and Bob said, "Is that your house?"
I said, "Yes, it is my house," and we went inside to play and have fun.

Dennis Milne (9)
Bervie School, Montrose

The Adventurer

Bill, the monster, wanted to explore the world
But how could he do it?
He ran around the city like a fox in the dark
And tried to find a boat.
He found a boat at the quayside and hid under the deck
He lived there for a long time
He lived off scraps and chased the rats
Finally, he felt a rumbling.
At last, they were off
But then the engine started to cough
He was having no luck
He would never get to travel the world
But then he saw a yacht
So shiny and silver
He walked inside and gasped
There was stuff from all around the world
Now he didn't have to travel the world
He jumped and twirled, he finally had his dream.

William Morris (9)
Bervie School, Montrose

Milles' Monster Adventure

Milles wants to explore the world, but he doesn't
Want to be seen, he goes inside a milkshake
Bottle to hide.
He jumps on a car
And goes far,
He meets a bin
His name was Bill.
They went on a boat to Egypt
And found a rock and some sticks inside
A pyramid, and then they saw
It move, they climbed into a vent to get away.
Suddenly, the rock said its name was Mr Rock,
He also wanted to help them explore the world.
Then they went on an aeroplane
To America and went in a drain.
They saw a scary monster they had
Heard about online, it was called Susone.
They decided to run onto the aeroplane
To get to Beijing.

Vinnie Walker (9)
Bervie School, Montrose

Hovering Holly

There was a girl in London
She bought some cotton candy
She took a bite
A monster jumped out
It said, "Hi, my name is Hovering Holly,"
Then *boom!* She was gone
It started to rain, but it was still sunny
Hovering Holly flew up to the sky
Where a rainbow had appeared
Another monster was on the rainbow
Their name was Liv and Dev
They slid down the rainbow
Then Hovering Holly flew away
She ended up in a mythical land
She found a giraffe and made a potion
It was a rainbow potion
She put it on the giraffe
The giraffe turned rainbow
She kept the giraffe as a pet.

Rebecca Rae (10)
Bervie School, Montrose

Monster Poetry - Creature Features

School Of Banban!

It was a nice day at the school of Banban
But there was a group of monsters
Talking in the classroom.
They were talking about turning all the kids into monsters
A kid overheard them and told everyone.
One of the monsters called Stinger Flynn
Left the room and grabbed the kid.
Stinger Flynn slid away with the stolen kid
The other monsters started to fight the other children.
Jumble Jon, the biggest monster,
Collapsed on all the monsters.
They all fell into the empty ball pit and disappeared
Never to be seen again.

Ivy Tait (10)
Bervie School, Montrose

The World

I went to the lab
To see what I could grab
When I saw the most peculiar thing
It was big and furry and loved to sing.
But was ever so scary like a giant hound
I thought I might show him around
I wandered for a bit
Then I got it
We should go around the world
We went to Japan and twirled
We went to Ukraine
We travelled with a plane
We got back to the lab
When the monster said, "That was as boring as a slab,
Let's never do that again."

Freya Wilson (9)
Bervie School, Montrose

Lady Glitter Sparkles

One day, on my way to school
I met a nice alien called Lady Glitter Sparkles
She was a shape-shifter
She told me she was from Planet Baba
It was destroyed by the Gorg
The Gorg was her worst enemy
Lady Glitter Sparkles burned all of the galaxy
Then she found Earth
Then we got to school
We had a lot of fun
After, we went to Cosmos
Then I got a guitar.
At the end of the day, she left
She said she would come back
She promised.

Emily Shaw (9)
Bervie School, Montrose

Physical Death Strikes

The monster, Physical Death, liked to visit castles
He travelled around the whole world
He was a scary, smelly, spooky monster
Who travelled with his friends.
He was from New Zealand
He liked to steal crowns and tiaras
But he never got caught
He kidnapped kings and queens.
Until he fell in love with
One of the king's daughters
He felt so happy
He destroyed the castles
He married the daughter
And he still travels the world.

Hannah Knights (9)
Bervie School, Montrose

Fairy Twinkle Toes

It was a lovely sunny day.
I was doing my homework in the classroom
When, suddenly, there was a big boom!
Then, suddenly, Fairy Twinkle Toes burst in
She was pink and fluffy.
When, suddenly, the bully came in.
Then the *bully* started bullying me!
And then Fairy Twinkle Toes stepped in
And then she used her magic and went
Bing, bong, boom!

Danielle Bagnall (10)
Bervie School, Montrose

The Plan

This is Sussy Baka 123 SCP 999
He is also known as Tubby Johnstone
With his red balloon.
His favourite food is roast beef
He loves to press 'emergency meeting' buttons every day.
Airship is his home
He sleeps in a giant cupboard
His giant plan is to conquer the world.
Well, that was nice
I'll do that again with you
Bye-bye.

Angus Jacobsen (9)
Bervie School, Montrose

The Terrifying Day

On a deserted day
I was bored
I saw a temple
I went in.
I saw Mr Rock.
He had two eyes.
He chased me
So, I began to run
I found light bright enough to stun
I pointed it at the monster
He dodged it
I had one battery left.
I shone it right at him
He died
He only wanted a friend.

Jaxon Lawrie (10)
Bervie School, Montrose

Bubbly

Bubbly is a little bubble
That *loooves* a snuggle.
She went down to Earth to get
Some people and met
Mia, then they went on a walk and came across a net.
They stopped by the beach
And saw a leech.
They decided to have a picnic.
Bubbly nicked the last sandwich.
They made good friends.

Mia Rae (9)
Bervie School, Montrose

The Fiddle

The Fiddle is a naughty creature
That creeps and crawls around.
He is known as a sheep
To those who see him and creak
But, in truth, he is a monster
So sly and slick and sleek
To everyone he knows
He is known as a freak.

Ayana Van Rooyen (10)
Bervie School, Montrose

Fluffy Fire Ball

Once, there was a monster called Fluffy Fire Ball,
She was very good at making up jokes during nightfall.
She was going to a joke competition,
She was certainly hoping for first position!
Fluffy Fire Ball was up against the king
He was very good at everything
So, I told her not to be shy
Because the king is a very nice guy
Fluffy Fire Ball did her thing
Then, up next was the king
His joke made everybody feel his grace
So then he came first place
Fluffy Fire Ball was quite mad.
But, on the other hand, the king was quite glad.
Fluffy Fire Ball exploded into a fierce little creature
She acted as strict as a teacher
So, I told her to calm down
As she stamped her feet against the ground
She started to calm down, so, as a reward

The king gave her a very nice award
She told a good joke that created a lot of laughter
Then everybody lived happily ever after.

Nellie Branagan (9)
Gorsey Bank Primary School, Wilmslow

Devil Danger

One day, I met a guy,
Who sometimes can be a bit sly
All that he wishes is to only
Have some money, he's lonely
You've not heard his laughter
Or seen his smile after
The start of his first day
His spaceship crashed and he has to stay
His legs are insanely long
And, sadly, people call him wrong
Inside, he's a very sweet
Kind of guy and he loves company as a treat
He has always had a hard
Life and has to sleep in someone else's yard
One day, when he got up, he heard a shout
It was someone calling for him to get out
Of their lawn, he's getting prepared
To get his ship repaired
He's trying to make a partnership
The only problem is, he's not got good workmanship

He's going to an incredible place
His home is deep in space
His name is Devil Danger
And he could be your saviour.

Oliver Conoley (9)
Gorsey Bank Primary School, Wilmslow

Bluey Viking Stopped Teachers From Striking

There once was a creature,
That became a teacher!
He was called Bluey Viking,
Who stopped teachers from striking,
He had a lot of friends,
That came over on weekends,
Bluey Viking is sometimes shy,
But is a very nice guy,
He moved to a new school,
Which has a very delightful pool,
He loved to run,
But medals he never won,
He is very woolly,
And only sometimes a bully,
Then he found a girl,
Who did a very cute twirl,
He instantly fell in love,
And her he didn't shove,
She joined him, being a teacher,

And that's how a girl married a creature,
All the children loved her,
They gave a small purr,
Together, they had lots of laughter,
And they lived happily ever after.

Beatrice Mellor (8)
Gorsey Bank Primary School, Wilmslow

Pop To The Shops

Me and my pet monster, Tiny, wanted to go to the shops,
We headed there and all we did was hop.
The first shop we entered was the potion one,
Tiny ate a bun.
He also drank a potion,
Which made him walk in slow motion.
Next, we went to the glasses store because Tiny's
Eyesight is bad,
When I asked him to put the glasses on, he looked
A little bit mad.
Eventually, he put them on and said he was having
A ball,
I asked why and he explained he could see through walls.
We headed home and saw a shop that had King Charles' face in,

We went and bought a mask, it was such a bargain.
We went home and got ready for bed,
I whispered to Tiny, "It's time to rest our heads."

Charlotte Gay (8)
Gorsey Bank Primary School, Wilmslow

Monster Chaos

One morning, I woke up and looked under my bed,
There was a monster that was red.
I said, "Will you come to school with me?"
But, like I thought, he didn't agree.
Then I saw it was a strike day,
Suddenly, the monster ran away.
I found him being the teacher,
Everyone shouted, "Who is this hairy creature?"
The head teacher found him,
So, the monster said, "Do you know where I can go for a swim?"
I had a busy day at school,
And the monster said that was so cool.
"I know you would want to come,
Next time, you can try playing the drum."
"Yes, but it is time for me to go home,
Let's get some ice cream first, I'm going to get honeycomb."

Till Knight (9)
Gorsey Bank Primary School, Wilmslow

Grogu

Once upon a time, a monster named Grogu
Was friendly and kind, with a big green hue.
He went to meet King Charles, with a smile so wide.
But manner and etiquette he couldn't abide.
He made a mistake and was a bit rude,
He didn't mean to start a feud.
With a wave goodbye, he left in his spaceship
And set off on an adventure, for a fun trip.
Exploring the galaxy, he met creatures new
Some big, some small, some red, some blue
But Grogu remembered his manners, as polite as can be
And learnt that manners are polite for you and me
To this day, he's still flying
Above us, trying
To discover the universe
Once he's done his mission, he'll be a nurse.

Jake Woods (9)
Gorsey Bank Primary School, Wilmslow

My Creature

Once, there was a little creature
Who loved his teacher
Every time she was on strike,
He would bike
His way to the shops
To get her some Pop Rocks.
Once he got to her house, he'd give her them
The teacher's name was Clem.
The creature would bike his way back
And give himself a pat on the back.
Once he got back, his mum said, "That was a very nice thing.
You should bring
Her some more."
"Okay, Mum,
I will bring her some."
"But tomorrow you're not in.
Wait, put that packet of Pop Rocks in the bin.
Okay, you can tell Clem
That you're bringing them
On Monday."

Romy Cliff (9)
Gorsey Bank Primary School, Wilmslow

Monster Poetry - Creature Features

Bob's Story At Playtime

Once, there was a monster called Bob
All he wanted was just a job
Until the end of the day, all he wanted was a friend with which to play
So, he went to school and asked a lonely person sitting on hay
He said, "Sure, what do you want to do?"
Bob said, "Oh, you want to do something new?"
He said, "Yes, let's play tig,"
When Bob saw him wearing a wig!
They had loads of laughter
Bob even got more friends after.
Some people said Bob was a fool
But his friends say they're just cruel
He loved his friends so much
Bob clutched his friends with a little touch.

Albie Croston (8)
Gorsey Bank Primary School, Wilmslow

A Monster Came To My School!

Once, a monster came to my fantastic school,
I thought it was awesome, very cool,
Other people thought and would be terrified,
That just made him completely horrified,
He had a fear of people, so he was really shy,
But he was a very charming guy,
He was a colossal, huge and loving fool,
When he was at my pleasant school,
I thought he should be a teacher,
My friend said, "No, he's a mysterious creature."
This decision is super-duper tricky,
But it is funny when he's sticky,
He said he isn't from this place,
I gasped and said, "Space?"

Sam Walton (8)
Gorsey Bank Primary School, Wilmslow

Cuddles And The Bay

There was once lots of plastic in the bay,
And Cuddles wanted to save the day.
He wasn't doing this all for grace,
And he really was from outer space.
Cuddles always had a good heart,
And his favourite thing to do was art.
He had always been extremely fluffy,
And always very, very scruffy.
Cuddles was always a delight,
And kind and polite.
Cuddles goes to the bay twice a week,
To remove the plastic and make it sleek.
In the end,
Our friendship can't descend.
There is still lots of plastic in the bay,
And you can help Cuddles save the day!

Holly Hosie (9)
Gorsey Bank Primary School, Wilmslow

A Monster Came To School

One day, it was the holidays and I found a
Curious creature,
No one could believe what I found
Especially the teacher.
I asked, "Where are you from?" and
It was space,
I asked again, "Why did you come to
This place?"
He told me, "It's very sunny,"
And I couldn't believe he was actually
Funny.
At times, he could be scary,
But he was usually just hairy.
He really wanted to make friends
And would want to build really
Good dens.
He makes really good laughter,
So we lived happily ever after.

William Goffredo (9)
Gorsey Bank Primary School, Wilmslow

My Monster

My monster is called John,
His favourite animal is a swan,
One day, John wanted to come,
To the park and he won,
The race down the slide,
But then I sadly sighed,
John then said, "Let's go to school,"
So I took John to school and he didn't follow the rules,
John has quite a big lung,
And he has a blue long tongue,
He was very annoyed because he couldn't eat his dinner,
John went to a competition and he was the winner,
Now, every day, I can have a nice day at school,
And sometimes have a relax in the pool.

Bobby McCamley (8)
Gorsey Bank Primary School, Wilmslow

Strike Went Wrong!

One day, there was a school strike and I had no teacher
Unexpectedly, he was replaced with a clumsy creature.
He was very clueless
Walking around shoeless!
It was time for first break and it was going to be fun
Because of the bright sun.
We played together
Little time went by but it felt like forever.
We ended the day with laughter
And we all lived happily ever after.
The monster was having a hard time being a teacher
He just wanted to be his own creature.
If only teachers got paid fairly
This would only happen very rarely.

Amelie Hargreaves (9)
Gorsey Bank Primary School, Wilmslow

Monstrous Monster

The monster, Mike Monster, that's me
I love to eat junk food and tea
I always have an enormous wee
On my street.
I dribble and drool all over me
It looks like it's time for a shopping spree
It's safe to say I've got a big knee
My knee is much bigger than a bee
It looks like it's time to go because I need
To wee
I love my green sweets so that I have a
Green knee
Great, I've landed on Planet Burgers
The burgers grow on trees, but the rivers are
Wee
At least the ocean is made from tea.

Leo Munsch (9)
Gorsey Bank Primary School, Wilmslow

Blue Blob

There was once a monster whose
Name was Blue
He was very scary, it is true
He went to school
He said, "School is not cool
And it is not the thing
For me." He said, "I am going to be the king
When I grow up," but
No luck
He was from space
And, "I like this place
And I am going to stay here forever
Because I am very clever.
My teacher said I need to do my maths
But I am going to do my maths in the bath."
He said to his friends,
Would they like to come on the weekend?

Madeleine Boardman (9)
Gorsey Bank Primary School, Wilmslow

My Monster Poem

There was once a teacher
Who was replaced by a creature
The teacher got depressed
But the children got obsessed
He said something funny
Then the story turned sunny
From that day on, they were friends
They saw each other most weekends
He was very kind
He had a very smart mind
It was the best day of school
I just wanted to jump into a pool
He could pretend he was sad
But he was just being bad
He could turn himself into a square
But he has to be careful that he doesn't get sat on like a chair.

Darcy Dick (9)
Gorsey Bank Primary School, Wilmslow

My Mad Replacement Creature

One day, I had no teacher,
Unexpectedly, he was replaced by a creature,
It was a monster that was hairy,
Very tall and really scary,
All of us were highly curious,
But if we talked, he would get furious,
When he asked us a question,
We would always have to make a suggestion,
If you don't get an answer right,
It will be a frightening sight,
If he opens his mouth, it will be sticky,
If you want to recover, it will be tricky,
At the end of the day, he said, "*Get out*,"
With a shout.

Jack Shuttleworth (9)
Gorsey Bank Primary School, Wilmslow

The Revenge Of The Monster

There was once a creature,
He was an enormous feature,
Everyone thought he was a nice one,
But he went to a house and broke an intercom,
He was now on a spree,
Mayor Bob used the special key
To lock the wall,
But he gobbled it down and grew very tall!
He had a big tongue
And licked the mayor but, still, he grew long.
He went wild,
(He definitely wasn't mild!)
He stole a blue
Banner and broke a pool cue,
Everyone now thought he was horrid,
Now he's a big monster so mean and torrid.

Henry Jones (9)
Gorsey Bank Primary School, Wilmslow

He Went To The Park

Slimebob was sticky, slurpy and shy,
But he's a very nice guy.
He is very funny,
And so is his bunny.
He was born on a planet called Ickysticky,
And, for him, life has been so tricky.
He's got no friends and is so lonely,
He'd love a mate. Oh, if only.
He went to the park,
And collected bark,
People said he was a fool,
But he wasn't cruel.
Now everyone wanted to be his friend,
They all hung out most weekends.
They had lots of laughter,
Happily ever after.

Arabella Durow (9)
Gorsey Bank Primary School, Wilmslow

Candy-Floss

Candy-floss looks only four,
Candy-floss can't reach the door.

Candy-floss is very small,
Candy-floss, you're about to fall.

Candy-floss I met in my dreams when I was asleep,
Candy-floss gave me the freaks.

I took Candy-floss to school and we did art,
But, annoyingly, it would never start!

A monster took over, surprise,
Candy-floss and the new teacher were very alike.

And, after school, we had supper,
Then she flew back on a magic scooter.

Zarrah Sardar (9)
Gorsey Bank Primary School, Wilmslow

My Monster

There once was a monster named Serious Steve.
What he got up to you wouldn't believe
He goes into school and causes havoc
And all the children panic.
He made some children cry by throwing pies.
He stole bags
And he always gets mad.
He throws pencils and makes himself glad.
He really is quite bad.
He makes all the children sad.
He smashed glass
And it covered the grass.
The teacher wasn't sad
He was very, very *mad!*
They called him Serious Steve.

Rupert Burnham (9)
Gorsey Bank Primary School, Wilmslow

Monster Poetry - Creature Features

One Strike Day

One day, it was strike day, we had no teacher,
But I snuck in a huge invisible creature.
He was a bit of a fool
But he was not cruel,
He got stuck in glue
And he was not blue.
He taught the class and then the bully
Got turned into a big wally
He said to me, "Earth is a place
I like but my home is in space!
Now, because I messed with glue, I'm sticky
This one strike day is going to be tricky
Today, I taught another class
It's like an overpass!"

Elliott Cartwright (9)
Gorsey Bank Primary School, Wilmslow

My Monster

The monster was evil and sad,
But his dad was glad!
He wanted to fly,
He was a spy!
He wanted to climb,
But he caused a crime!
He didn't have time,
He got stuck in slime!
He was in a house,
With a mouse!
He wanted to kick,
A brick!
He tried to flick,
Some chicks!
He wanted to pour water,
On his daughter!
He was a king,
And people needed to sing!
He was fat,

He found a bat!
He was scary,
And ate a cherry!

Nigel Man (9)
Gorsey Bank Primary School, Wilmslow

The Monster That Came To School

Once, there was a monster that was quite scary,
People also thought he was hairy,
One day, he met a fool,
Who wasn't cruel,
But wanted to take him to school,
His friends thought he was cool,
But when the teacher saw, she said, "*Out!*"
With a booming and deafening shout,
He was so very sad,
He went super mad,
He wanted to go to his happy home,
So he could only roam,
He got on his majestic ship,
And went off with a zip!

Leo Wiltshire (9)
Gorsey Bank Primary School, Wilmslow

Monster Poetry - Creature Features

The Creature Who Wanted To Meet My Teacher

One day, as I woke,
I hardly spoke!
For, right in front of me, was a creature,
Who said he wanted to meet my teacher!
I took him to school with me,
Sadly, we had to stop for a wee!
My friends wanted to peek
And my monster gave a squeak!
I told them not to tell a soul
Or they would find themselves sick in a bowl!
I slowly took him out,
And he had a loud shout,
And he curled up into a ball,
While another monster came out the wall!

Jenson Higby (9)
Gorsey Bank Primary School, Wilmslow

The White Monstrosity

There was one day where I brought my
Monster into school.
He made me look like such a fool.
The teacher was surprised, "What is this creature?"
Asked the teacher.
"Is it from space?
And how did it get to this place?"
He started flipping things over, being
A disgrace!
The teacher shouted, "Get out and
Go back to outer space!"
He didn't want to stop
And then he had a big plop.

Skyla George (9)
Gorsey Bank Primary School, Wilmslow

The Imaginative Monster, Mo

One day, I woke early to see a monster under my bed,
He had yellow ears on top of his head.

Two orange tongues,
And bright purple lungs.

I imagine his rose-red eyes staring at me,
As I lie in bed and cuddle my teddy.

On top of my bed, sometimes if I dare,
I'll try to spy my monster under there.

He said to me, late at night,
"I am not at school because there are monster strikes!"

Clara Stockdill (9)
Gorsey Bank Primary School, Wilmslow

Hop To The Shops

This morning, when I got out of bed,
I saw a monster wanting bread.

We decided we wanted to hop,
And I said, "Let's go to the shop."

When we arrived, we saw a crown,
And nobody had a frown!

We wondered why, so I looked at the news,
There was a coronation and they didn't let us choose!

We found the bread we were looking for,
And it turns out, the fluffy monster wanted more!

Alexandra Martin (8)
Gorsey Bank Primary School, Wilmslow

Monster's Life

There was a monster called Billy.
He was a little bit silly.
He is a bit of a fool.
If he gets angry, he will be cruel.
He is dry.
But if some day he is slimy, he will cry.
He is a bit smelly
He will fight you with a welly.
He is a bit sticky.
He is a bit tricky.
He is on his own only.
So, he is lonely.
I asked, "What place?"
He said, "I am from space."

Lucas Wright (9)
Gorsey Bank Primary School, Wilmslow

There's A Monster Under My Bed!

There's a monster under my bed and I don't know what to do,
I heard a nasty screeching noise, so I ran to the loo.

He banged and he crashed on the wooden toilet door,
Then, one time, he hit so hard I fell onto the floor.

He was green, slimy and pretty sticky,
With one look I knew this day would be tricky.

They said sorry and pulled me up,
And flew back to Planet Gluck.

Leo Ritchie (9)
Gorsey Bank Primary School, Wilmslow

Shape-Shifter Bob

One day, I woke up,
I found a monster asking for a cup.

I said, "No, no, no, what do you want to do?"
He said, "I want to build a universe with you."

I said, "We can't do that, we'll disappear,
The King's coronation is about to appear.

We can't miss that, we'll live in fear,
So, let's celebrate the King and cheer!"

Archie Jones (9)
Gorsey Bank Primary School, Wilmslow

Friends With Fuzz

One day, when I was awake,
I saw a monster eating a rake.

He said, "I want to go to school."
I replied, "I'll take you there since it's very cool."

I showed my friend and the fun didn't end.
He made dens out of pens!

Then I said, "We can't come again because there are strikes,
We'll just have to fly our kite."

Robyn Howard (9)
Gorsey Bank Primary School, Wilmslow

The Monster In The Park

Last night, I went to the park,
When I saw something in the dark,

It was a weird sort of beast,
That wanted a feast.

So, I took him to my house,
And saw him trying to catch a mouse!

It was soon time for bed,
When I saw him resting above my head.

I woke in the morning but he had disappeared,
Which I thought was a bit weird.

Olivia Mainwaring (9)
Gorsey Bank Primary School, Wilmslow

The Day A Frilled Beast Came

This morning, I woke up,
Something threw a cup.

So, I ran into my loo,
There was a monster eating shampoo.

So, I took him to school, nearly everybody screamed,
But my teacher gleamed.

The creature,
Ate my teacher.

I went to bed,
And cuddled my ted.

Next morning, it had vanished,
As if it was banished.

Frederick Hitch (9)
Gorsey Bank Primary School, Wilmslow

School Strike Day

I woke up and opened my wardrobe,
There was a monster wearing my robe!

He was wearing a delicious chocolate snack,
From his rucksack.

"Do you need to go to school?
Is it very fun and cool?"

"No, it is strike day,
Let's go and play!"

"We need to go to bed,
Don't bang your head."

Jacob Beetson (9)
Gorsey Bank Primary School, Wilmslow

Hug Blaze

There once was a monster called Blaze,
He lived in an egg which he called Haze,
He visited the volcano to swim in the lava,
His egg almost broke, what a palaver!
He had a pet chicken that Blaze was always licking
Then he ate ice cream and shared it with a scream
Blaze had a good day, so he slept in hay
He fell asleep counting sheep.

Zainuddin Ahmed (8)
Gorsey Bank Primary School, Wilmslow

Scaly Scyper

I woke up and opened my wardrobe,
Inside, a monster was spinning my globe.

Me and him hopped to the shop
After he said, "I want a lollipop."

He saw a cool potion
And he drank it in slow motion.

Unfortunately, the monster said, "I want to go home,"
So, I flew him back on a pile of foam.

Charlie Manton (9)
Gorsey Bank Primary School, Wilmslow

Little Monster

My little monster came one day
My little monster came to stay
She's evil on the inside, but
Cute on the out
I took her to gymnastics
She said it was fantastic
It was time for dinner now,
She said it tasted like plastic
I think she was being sarcastic
What Little Monster does for fun
Is bathe in the sun.

Poppy Favour (9)
Gorsey Bank Primary School, Wilmslow

The Monster In My Room

One morning, I couldn't believe my eyes,
There was a monster eating some pies.

It said hello, I said it back,
Then he told me he was looking for another snack.

I decided to take him down the stairs,
Then I realised he had my teddy bears.

Suddenly, he bumped his head,
Then I realised he was dead!

Jude Wolstenholme (9)
Gorsey Bank Primary School, Wilmslow

Choco

There's a monster in my bed,
And it's eating chocolate spread.

We went to school this morning,
And got a little warning,

It would cause a lot of pain,
But no need to worry because it's going to rain.

It's time to go back to his planet,
And he's flying back on a giant mallet.

Kaasim Khaliq (9)
Gorsey Bank Primary School, Wilmslow

Little Monster

Once, there was a little monster
Who went to school
And acted cool.
She was really a fool
Not trying to be cruel
She really needed a tool
And she kicked a pool
One day, it was school
She got a pool after school.
She jumped in and felt like
A fool.
The next day, she felt
Cool.

Neve Atkinson (9)
Gorsey Bank Primary School, Wilmslow

Evil Chopper

Once, there was a monster that was quite a fool,
But people thought he was cruel,
A boy wanted to take him to school,
And people thought he was cool,
When the teacher saw him,
She said, "Out!"
With a shout
He was so sad
He went mad
He went out of school,
And found a jewel.

Hugo Ashurst (9)
Gorsey Bank Primary School, Wilmslow

Anger

One day, there was a creature,
Who sat down on his teacher!
The creature was a monster,
And he eats lobster.
He is scary,
And he is hairy!
He has big, fat lungs,
And he has a green tongue,
He always sets a scene
He is very, very mean!
He is quite fat
I can't believe that!

Thomas O'Shea (8)
Gorsey Bank Primary School, Wilmslow

Naughty Nora

I woke up one day,
To find a monster in my way,

He was so cute, so I looked after him,
Sadly, he fell and broke his limb.

So, I took him with me,
And the teacher said, "Let the creature be."

Then I took him home and put him in a jar,
Right next to my old guitar.

Jemima Langman (9)
Gorsey Bank Primary School, Wilmslow

Giant Shadow Comb

One day, I jumped out of my bed,
There was a monster straight ahead.

He said he wanted to go to the park,
Then we saw the new monarch.

He was so old,
And had millions of gold.

After, the monster said he had to go home,
Then he flew away on a giant comb.

Theo Clarke (8)
Gorsey Bank Primary School, Wilmslow

The Batter

One day, under my bed,
There was a monster with a big head.

I asked if he wanted to come to the cricket with me,
But, instead, he had a cup of tea!

Let's watch the coronation
With the rest of the nation.

As he flew back,
He had a very quick snack.

Alfie Little (9)
Gorsey Bank Primary School, Wilmslow

Charlottena's Day Out

One morning, under my bed,
I saw a monster eating some bread.

So, I took her to the park,
She started to pick off some bark.

We saw the new king walking his dogs,
Then she was standing on some logs!

Sadly, she had to go,
Luckily, it was only for a mo!

Lucy Loughhead (9)
Gorsey Bank Primary School, Wilmslow

I Found A Monster Under My Bed!

This morning, I found a monster under my bed.
When I looked closely, she was eating some bread.

I said, "Have you got any special powers?"
And, suddenly, my room was covered in flowers!

I realised I was late for school,
And then she flew to the local pool.

Sophie Sharman (9)
Gorsey Bank Primary School, Wilmslow

Mischievous Monster

There's a monster under my bed, I don't know what to do.
So, I said, "Who are you?"
He was blue
While chewing on bamboo.
He was hungry, so I gave him a meal,
And I saw him nibbling on eel.
I rushed to the loo
And I didn't know what to do.

Aston Tyler (9)
Gorsey Bank Primary School, Wilmslow

The Creature Under My Bed

This morning, I heard a bang under my bed.
Something had hit its head.

It was a creature
That was apparently an amazing teacher
It had come to be a bleacher.

He was not at work because he was striking
I sat in bed and watched it act like a Viking.

James Aughton (9)
Gorsey Bank Primary School, Wilmslow

Drop Bear Fail

One morning, I saw a creature in the tree,
Like one huge hairy flee.

It stared at me with its mammoth eyes,
They were so enormous, they could fit in some pies.

Suddenly, it launched at me and hit the window,
And then it landed on a pillow.

Benjamin Shaw (9)
Gorsey Bank Primary School, Wilmslow

Boo!

This morning, I saw a monster under my bed,
So, I gave it a piece of my bread.

I said, "Do you want to go to school?
You'll need to follow all the rules."

Its name is Boo,
It likes to scare me and you.

Jamie Wong (8)
Gorsey Bank Primary School, Wilmslow

Hairy Scary

One morning, I saw a creature in a tree,
He fell out and hit a pea.

I came out into the garden to help him,
It turned out he had broken his limb.

But it healed in one second,
It's time for bed, I reckon.

William Graham (9)
Gorsey Bank Primary School, Wilmslow

Mysterious Monster

This morning, I woke up,
I went to get my cup.

Then a monster was up in a tree,
I told my mum, but she didn't agree.

We looked out of the window, but he was not there,
Then I saw him hugging a bear.

Tom Davies (8)
Gorsey Bank Primary School, Wilmslow

Monster Poetry - Creature Features

Monster Madness

One day, I woke up,
Looked out of my window

I saw a monster,
He was mad.

He was jumping to the shelf,

He was still mad.
So he ran to the bedroom.

Hanoch Rino (8)
Gorsey Bank Primary School, Wilmslow

Monster Poem

One day, I woke up and I saw something,
A monster on a swing.

It was red,
And lived under my bed.

It was really small,
Then I had a fall.

Olivia Bauer (9)
Gorsey Bank Primary School, Wilmslow

Monster Madness

Meet Scarie, you'll be scared so slightly,
With his textured belly and his bouncy vocals.
Yet he loves designs, most likely because he can see sound and
Hear colours.
He is very annoying
I took him to school.
Instead, he went to the pool.
He thought it was as cool as a cucumber
He thinks he's as hot as a Harry Potter film
He finally left the pool and went to school.
"Sit down," said my teacher, Mrs Brown
Then Scarie asked if we could watch Mary Poppins JR,
"Yes," said Mrs Brown, "of course we can."
He lit a candle and it came...
He turned into a fire-breathing
Heartbreaking dragon.

Niamh Hackett (9)
Hermitage Primary School, Helensburgh

Mewbot Saves Her Community

There once was an ancient forest, that no one
Dared to ever forage.
As cute as a kitten but as deadly as a demon,
A dangerous creature lurked.
A crash! And a bang!
And there it was, a legendary cyborg cat.

Mewbot and the cunning cyborg cat once broke into a massive
Fight!
Millions of humans came to watch,
Mewbot pushed her community away
And they turned angry and sad.

Mewbot moved to the zoo,
She hoped people would like her too.
She was as kind as a rabbit but still a little fierce.
She listened well with her metal ears.
There once was an ancient forest, and in that forest lived a
Beloved Mewbot.

Poppy Hall (8)
Hermitage Primary School, Helensburgh

Monster Poetry - Creature Features

Check Under Your Bed!

I got up to a cute and cuddly sight!
But did this thing want to fight?
Slowly, I tiptoed
Hoping I wasn't being followed.
I was going to Glasgow!
But how?
I've got a monster on my trail!
I'm going to fail!
I guess I need to bring him with me.
Here we are!
We've come so far!
Look over there!
A fair!
Oh, no!
Everybody is starting to go!
The kids start to weep.
Is Check, the monster, giving them the creep?
Check is a friendly thing!
He's got quite a strong *ding*!
Well, that was a fun day out!
Let's go before anyone starts to pout!

Georgia Dow (9)
Hermitage Primary School, Helensburgh

Messy Magic

One cold winter day, Confetti was performing a magic show
When Confetti was in the middle of his magical disappearing trick, it started to snow.
I was in my glittering seat which was as fluffy as a pillow.
Watch Confetti be as magic as a magician.
Suddenly, from out of his hat
Shot out a cat.
Just then, through the door ran in an insane Dalmation
Coming after him was a leaping lion.
They ran around the stage
Underneath a metal cage.
Before it got out of control, confident Confetti did his magic
And made the best of friends.

Nyla Troup (8)
Hermitage Primary School, Helensburgh

Sneaky Monster

One day, Sneaky was swimming in the ocean,
Catching slippery and slimy fish.
Sneaky was as fierce as a lion swimming in the spraying of the salty sea which was raging out.
Suddenly, he started going calmly by,
When a boat came.
My monster made a growl and ripped open the hull.
All the people went to see what had happened.
Then another boat came and they got into it.
Eventually, they reached the shore.
They saw the hideous and frightening Sneaky,
Finally, Sneaky drove the terrified people into the enormous and dangerous deep pit.

Ciaran McHardy (8)
Hermitage Primary School, Helensburgh

Go To Cuddle Island

One day, I was playing in my garden.
Then, suddenly, I saw a cute creature lying just behind me
I said hello, he said, "Do you want a hug?"
I said no, then we became friends.
He said his home was on Cuddle Island
And then I knew our mission was to go to Cuddle Island
Then he said thank you
Then he showed me a portal
We went through and he said we were immortal
It was so beautiful with cherry blossom trees all over
There, in the middle, was a hut with his family
He said goodbye and I went home.

Lewis Aitken (9)
Hermitage Primary School, Helensburgh

How My Monster Saved The World!

One day, a monster called Fuzzy Wusy came to my house.
She said that she needed help.

There is a mysterious monster living in a dark and damp cave.
She yelped...

So, we hopped into the flying monster mobile.
We zoomed and kaboomed,
Which was as big as two bouncy balls

We travelled to the cave to talk to the
Terrifying troll

Fuzzy Wusy bounced in and bit the troll's
Dirty machine

She then went into demon mode and bit
His dirty toe.

Katie Buchanan (8)
Hermitage Primary School, Helensburgh

My Day Out

On the way to the shops, I saw my friend
Buz.
I said hello to her.
She said hi back.
Buz asked if I wanted to go shopping with her.
And I said yes!

After that, we walked to the shops.
We went there and then went in.
We were both so hungry, so we got
McDonald's.
We finished the rest of the shopping and then
Went home.

After we got home, we had a pizza party.
After that, we had to have an end.
So, I said goodbye.
And that was that, was it.

Georgia Mccallion (9)
Hermitage Primary School, Helensburgh

Saving The Zoo

One sunny day, I was at the zoo,
When I saw a small fuzzy,
Sliding stupidly down the stairs.

She was as small as an avocado,
She told me that she wanted,
To free the zoo.

I told her, "Let's do it!"
So, when it was late, we slid around
On the cold, hard ground,
Trying to steal the rusty keys

We unlocked the cages
All of the thankful animals ran out
It was amazing.
I told Twinkle not to go,
She said we will meet again.

Charlotte Boyle (9)
Hermitage Primary School, Helensburgh

Monster Universe

One roasting-hot day,
I asked my evil monster friend from Australia,
If he wanted to play,
He said yes, so I got the food.
I went in my super speedy spaceship,
The spaceship was as speedy as a flash,
The monster was as tall as a giraffe
We blasted off to the moon.
Then I went to go get the food but…
It was missing
The monster was destroying the moon.
She was mad
I needed to drop her back off at Australia
I was really depressed.

Miller Hill (8)
Hermitage Primary School, Helensburgh

Rose Goes To School

My monster is Rose and it is her first day at school.
She is as beautiful as a rainbow,
And as cute as a kitten.
All my friends giggled and gaggled,
When Rose asked to go outside,
The teacher said yes.
She heard laughing and felt safe,
She touched her heart filled with love,
She smelled lunch,
She filled her tummy with lovely pizza,
Finally, it was time to go,
Rose will come back, I promised cheerfully.

Willow Muir (9)
Hermitage Primary School, Helensburgh

The Big Plot

On the way home, I met a monster
It was as tall as a skyscraper

His teeth were as sharp as spikes and as yellow as gold
He was as pale as a ghost, with hardly any neck

His desire was to conquer the world and eat everyone
But he was as dumb as a dinosaur

In the end, as the sun went down
He ended up conquering the world and eating everyone!

John Edwardson (8)
Hermitage Primary School, Helensburgh

Fig

One day, I woke up
I saw a massive monster
He was in the kitchen
And eating all the jam
He got a fright
And held onto me tight
I pushed him away
And told him not to stay
I thought that was the end until there was a bang on the door
I couldn't believe I saw a dinosaur standing on the floor.

Harlow McKenna (8)
Hermitage Primary School, Helensburgh

The Red Fluff Ball

One day, there was a little fluff ball
And, the next day, it was alive
It started turning red
It had two legs and two arms and hands
A few months later
That wee fluff ball became my friend
And I brought him on my holiday
We had so much fun together
Sadly, I had to keep him a secret from my parents.

Kyle Welsh (8)
Hermitage Primary School, Helensburgh

Monster Poetry - Creature Features

Ruaraidh The Adventurer

We met at my house for the adventure.
My dad drove us to the fearsome forest.
We got out of the car, suddenly it became as
Cold as the ocean.
It got dark, we heard some footsteps.
It was running, going as fast as fire.
It was my dad.
We were late.
It was funny.

James Wightwick (9)
Hermitage Primary School, Helensburgh

Pippy

Pippy is as cute as a puppy
Pippy met me at Tony's pizza shop
Pippy likes the totally tremendous tomatoes
Pippy heard people making noise,
Pippy could smell our perfect pizzas cooking
Pippy loves the pizza sign ruby red and yummy yellow
Pippy loves you all!

Olivia-Jo Cameron (8)
Hermitage Primary School, Helensburgh

Shopping Spree

One morning, me and my monster went in the car
Hope was her name
She was as cute as a kitten
We were shopping for food
We bought perfectly pretty pizzas
They were as round as a ball
We were stuffed full
So we had to nap.

Caris Reilly (8)
Hermitage Primary School, Helensburgh

Me And My Monster

One day, I was walking in a forest, the trees were green,
When I saw a monster, he said he wasn't mean.
He was as blue as the ocean.
He was so tall and fluffy.
He has one eye.
There was a patch on him.
It was a heart shape.
It was red, as red as a rose.
He said he was kind, as kind as can be.
So, I said, "Why don't we go to a tea party?"
So, we went on a bus, no one else was there, it was Just us.
But when we got there,
There was not tea.
We were really sad.
So, I said, "Why don't we climb a tree,
Instead of a tea party?"
The monster said, "Yes, but do you know my name?"
"No, but I bet it is the best," I said.

"It's Melow, by the way."
We climbed the highest tree, what happened next?
Well, you'll have to see.

Penny Turner (9)
Kirknewton Primary School, Kirknewton

Harmony The Monster Saves The Day!

Harmony, the monster, zigzags across the sky
Her silky, soft fur so dainty
She has no fur out of place.
Her eyes as bright
As gold.
Her wings as white as snow.
And if you're lucky, you may spot a glimpse of this elegant monster.
Her enemy, Witchy, is as quick as a flash
So mean, so cruel
What could I do?
Harmony thought, then thought some more,
I will go to the lake and fetch some glimmering glass water
She was back in a flash with a bucket of water filled to
The brim.
Then threw it over green Witchy, then she crumbled away.
"Yay!" shouted everyone!

Grace McNee (8)
Kirknewton Primary School, Kirknewton

Monster Poetry - Creature Features

The Monsters Came To My School!

One day, two monsters came to school,
One was called Lilypad.
She had webbed feet and webbed hands.
She also had reed-like hair, a leaf dress and a giant Lilypad sat atop her head.
The other monster had eyes as orange as fire and
A dark body as blue as the sea.
He was called Twilight,
Twilight was not nice.
He bullied everyone at my school.
And pushed everyone out of the swimming pool.
Lilypad just had enough and shouted, "Stop being mean!"
Suddenly, the monster crumbled into dust and disappeared.
Then everybody cheered!
I hope Lilypad comes back one day.

Lily Scallon (9)
Kirknewton Primary School, Kirknewton

Friends And Foes

Once upon a time, there was a dragon called
Draco the dragon.
Draco was as green as a turtle.
Draco was my best friend.
I would ride on his scaly back.
We always visited Cloud Island
(Cloud Island is where Draco is from)
And Earth.
Until we had a mighty fallout.
We fought fiercely and frowned.
We were like bombs about to burst with madness.
Until I stopped us and we finally forgave each other.
We had an awesome time like we used to.
It's much more fun to be friends than foes.
You will find that too!

Martha Bowman (9)
Kirknewton Primary School, Kirknewton

Making A New Friend

Many, many moons ago, there was a little girl
She was left out every day, especially at school
I hope you can keep a secret because this is
Quite a big one.
I am the monster that changed that girl's life.
One day, I knocked on that girl's door.
When she answered it, I asked her if she
Would like to play.
Oh, how she shouted, "Okay!"
You could hear her from
A mile away.
I spread my transparent wings and she hopped onto
My back.
We soared into the black.

Esther Shaw (9)
Kirknewton Primary School, Kirknewton

The Monster Hammerhead Shark

He is a sharp swimmer, twisting and turning.
Blue and pink and as spiky as anything.
Shooting out of the water and disappears.
Lots of people try to catch him but fail.
No one knows where he comes from, not even archaeologists.
He lives in a rocky cave, waiting for dinner to pass by.
Then he shoots and has his dinner.
He's the king of the ocean.
He is not scared of anything.
Except a *big* long whale!
He all turns blue and shoots into the undergrowth.

Ethan Cook (8)
Kirknewton Primary School, Kirknewton

Be Grateful For Your Life

Islay is a girl monster and is colourblind,
Even though she is colourblind,
She is not that different to everybody else.
Yes, some people bully her,
But she is happy with her life,
Because she knows that everyone is different
in their own way.
She used to hate her life, until her friends told
Her that everyone is different in their own way, so
Be grateful for your life and be grateful for your
friends.
Be grateful for your family and grateful you are
here.

Myla D'Arcy (9)
Kirknewton Primary School, Kirknewton

The Mohawk Warrior

On Saturday, I met a monster called Mohawk Warrior.
He's scary, vicious and mean.
He's 15ft 9.
He uses his mohawks as knives.
He has mohawks on his wings.
He cannot go to school because he's too big.
He's as red as lava.
He's the most powerful person in the World.
His mohawks are as black as space.
He has bright green eyes.
His tongue is bright yellow like a banana.
He is my friend.

Jack Watson (8)
Kirknewton Primary School, Kirknewton

Cozy The Candyfloss Monster

Cozy is a kind, cute monster.
She was born in a candyfloss cupboard.
Cozy has neon-pink eyes and light
Pink fur.
She has a best friend called Cleany.
Cozy was walking to the shops.
Then, suddenly, a big blue electric monster came
Out of nowhere.
Cozy ran off.
She told her mum.
Her mum was unhappy and she said, "Just
Ignore it."
And Cozy and her family lived happily
Ever after.

Laura Blain (9)
Kirknewton Primary School, Kirknewton

Detective Monster Bust

He has a friend snake that is helpful
He is good and kind, cool and helpful
He has a broken eye
He is a shape-shifter, he can turn into anything
He is a bat that cannot fly
He has four weapons that are so powerful
He is the strongest bat in the world
He is the fastest bat in the world
He has armour, it is the strongest armour in the world
His feet are so big, like the size of a bat.

Arwin Chawla (8)
Kirknewton Primary School, Kirknewton

Small Friends

This is Grape.
Grape is small
She wishes she was tall.
All the others are tall and mean
They crowd over her, she can't
Be seen.

Grape meets a monster even
Smaller than her.
They chat and chat and chat
They chat
About this and that

Small tells Grape that being
Little is still great, even
Though they were small, they are
A team.

Islay Mitchell (8)
Kirknewton Primary School, Kirknewton

Fluff Balls

On Sunday the 22nd of June, a teeny, tiny team of fluff balls were born,
In the Lollipop Forest on Nafalafagus.
One was slightly smaller than the rest.
She had a galaxy print all over her soft cloud-like body.
She was a space ball...
She was a chubby chunk of fluff.
And she was out to save the world.
First, she started to clean the beach.
Until it was as clean as a shark.

Charlotte Jack (8)
Kirknewton Primary School, Kirknewton

Electric King

Electric King is super scary.
He's the shape-shifter after me.
He's flying in the air at night,
He's swim-racing in the sea.
He wears his crown everywhere
Sometimes he takes it off.
He uses it like a weapon
His enemies go soft (on him).
I will catch him one day.
I will use the crown.
I will catch him in it.
I will take him down.

Finlay Nicol (8)
Kirknewton Primary School, Kirknewton

I Love Yellow

On Wednesday morning, the sun was
As bright as a light and as yellow
As a banana.
I love yellow because I am
As yellow as I can be.
Oh, I love yellow, I love
Lemons.
Too many lemons
Is excellent, but I get bullied
A lot because I am yellow.
But this is going to stop because I am
Strong, so strong
Wow, everyone
Is nice, yes.

Ailsa Goldie (8)
Kirknewton Primary School, Kirknewton

The Best Monster!

On a Thursday afternoon, a monster appeared.

She was called Marshmallow and she was so cute,
She had marshmallows in her tiny paws.

Marshmallow makes joy in rainbow clouds
When people are feeling down.

Marshmallow wants to make everyone happy
By making rainbows and making it rain
marshmallows!

Ellen Clark (8)
Kirknewton Primary School, Kirknewton

Cleanly

Cleanly was born in a cleaning
Cupboard, he is baby blue.

He has red spots on his nose.

Cleanly goes crazy.
He destroys all the buildings
He turns red and fire comes
Out his ears.

When I was cleaning, Cleanly looked
In my window

And he turned blue.
He cleaned everything.

Anabelle Jagla (9)
Kirknewton Primary School, Kirknewton

Mr Fluff

Once, when I was walking to school, I saw a Monster.
He was as white and fluffy as a cloud.
He looked about 5ft 5.
He said to me, "I was made by the God of Clouds
That's why I look like a cloud."
"Wowzers, wonderful," I said.
"When I am angry, I am as grey as clay," he said.

Emanuel Shiels (8)
Kirknewton Primary School, Kirknewton

Lonely

Ghosty is a boy monster
He is dyslexic and is four
He is based on me
He is lonely
He wants friends
He will later
He finds a friend
One week later
He sees a girl walk up to him
She asks if he wants to be her friend
He obviously says yes
One week later, they are BFFs.

Harris Blair (8)
Kirknewton Primary School, Kirknewton

My Playful Monster!

On Monday, I met my monster
His name is Slimy as Snot
He loved to play, so we played football.
He won but I don't care, I have a monster! And
I love him and he loves me.
We went to bed and slept and slept.
I love you, monster!

Natalie Berry (9)
Kirknewton Primary School, Kirknewton

All About My Monster, Cookie

Cookie was born in a cookie factory
Cookie became hungry all of a sudden
Cookie ate cookies, including himself
He is crumbly and colourful and ever so cute
He is a coloured blob
He is small.

Emma Dicker (9)
Kirknewton Primary School, Kirknewton

Hearty Helps

Hearty is colourful and fluffy
She is kind too.
She is from Unicorn Land
And
She helps.

Sophie Ward (9)
Kirknewton Primary School, Kirknewton

Naughty Monster!

There once was a monster,
His name was Bob,
The bad thing about him,
Is that he loved to rob,

One day, he robbed an ice cream van,
And carried what he could,
He slipped and slid in the streets,
Then ended up in mud,

He went to bed,
Bored of robbing,
And for the first time,
He started sobbing,

As being lonely,
He felt really sad,
About all the time,
He made people mad,

Then woke up,
Went to town,

Looked all around,
No friend was found,

So, off to the nearest city,
Looked around to find a job,
But the streets were too crowded,
Because of a big mob,

Although the mob was big,
It wasn't very scary,
Most of them had fake teeth,
And were very hairy,

Just then, he made a friend,
She was part of the mob,
Her name was Lavender,
So, they ran off together to find a new job!

Lydia Boome (8)
Ossett Holy Trinity CEVA Primary School, Ossett

Sally The Cheeky Monster

Sally is a cheeky monster who
Plays with all of her friends
Her friendship never ends.
She lives with her mum, Sophia,
Her dad, Samuel, and her sister, Stella.
And her BFF's name is Ella
And, right now, she's in Coachella,
Sending pictures all day long
Sally's phone going, *ping, ping, pong*,
She may be a bit small, but she has a *huge* heart
Which is full of love and laughter
From the top to the bottom,
Sally has a favourite hoppy black bunny
Which is her pet and her favourite hobby
Is to play out and paint with her family.

Katie Ibbetson (8)
Ossett Holy Trinity CEVA Primary School, Ossett

Wiggle Is A Friend

There's a monster named Wiggle, so bright and fun
He loves to play and dance in the sun
He wiggles and giggles, never sitting still
And his silly antics always bring a thrill

With his big googly eyes and his toothy grin
He'll make you laugh till your sides cave in
He loves to talk about his dreams
And wiggle through all his schemes

So, if you ever need a friend to make you smile
Just call Wiggle, he'll be there in a while
He'll bring his monster energy so wild and free
And wiggle his way into your heart, you'll see.

Hollie Roberts (8)
Ossett Holy Trinity CEVA Primary School, Ossett

Fang The Monstrous

Welcome to Planet Monster World
The home to Fang, the soft, sharp-toothed monster
He has a straight antennae, but
Sometimes it's curled
He has a million friends, he's still
The best dancer

Fang is very bad

He plans to destroy Planet Earth
This made the little girl sad
So, she needs to teach him his worth
When Fang came, the girl tried, but it
Didn't go well
Then she got the hang of it
She finally taught the monster
So, they became best friends forever.

Evelyne Croft (8)
Ossett Holy Trinity CEVA Primary School, Ossett

Fred The Monster

There once was a monster called Fred,
Who had red hair on his head,
His look was quite scary,
Even to his wife, Mary,
So, she made him put a hat on instead.

Fred had five eyes on his head,
He took them out before bed,
He was as blind as a bat,
Can you imagine that?
In the morning, he found pants on his head!

Thomas Milnes (8)
Ossett Holy Trinity CEVA Primary School, Ossett

Oogly Boogly

Monsters, monsters, furry and unfriendly
Looking quite lonely and going, going, going
Not knowing
What to do.
Acting very sweet.
Saying, "I am very, very hungry," looking in
The dirty, dirty bin
With a banana skin
On his head and being
Very crazy.
Looking at me
Like I am a funny-looking fool.

Hettie Walters (7)
Ossett Holy Trinity CEVA Primary School, Ossett

Kraken

Lurking deep, deep, deep under the sea
A submarine spots the Kraken,
And begins to flee.
As they struggle-ruggle to escape
Fish swim away in fright
The Kraken catches up and
Takes a bite
The Kraken roars in pure
Rage in the middle of their fight
At night.

Alex Ciobanu (7)
Ossett Holy Trinity CEVA Primary School, Ossett

The Flying Monster

In the night sky, he peeks around the tree's trunks
To find his aim to kill human beings.
So he has control of the whole world.
"Why would a wiggly, twiggy, little giant do such a thing?" most people ask.
Other people say, "It's a monster, they're angry and mean
Goofy and not very clean."
If you took a chance of being an owner of one
It would be worse than watching Peppa Pig for five days straight.

Dexter Jones (8)
Our Lady Of The Assumption Primary School, Belle Vale

The Invasion

Once upon a time
There was a monster who committed crime.
His name is Caleb,
He shall possess Saleb.
He has a stitch,
He lives in a ditch.
He gets onto a ship
To have a fun trip.

While he invades,
He plays charades.
"Earth's fun
Now I have to run.
I like this game, I'm gonna decide
I made up my mind..."

Owen Barnes (7)
Our Lady Of The Assumption Primary School, Belle Vale

Purple And Pink

Purple and Pink is a monster from Spain
Who does not like to cause any pain!
Purple and Pink can cause quite a stink
With her funny wink.
She has four arms and legs
And stinks of eggs.
With nightmare fangs that cause a scare.
But Purple and Pink is fluffy and sweet
But she stinks of feet.

Amelie Gorman (8)
Our Lady Of The Assumption Primary School, Belle Vale

Monster-Bonster

Little Miss Hobnob was
Silly and frilly
She liked to rob
To feed her gob.
She robbed a Coke
And began to choke.
She had crazy eyes
Which looked like pies
And funny teeth
Which smelled of beef.

Ava Gorman (8)
Our Lady Of The Assumption Primary School, Belle Vale

Menace

M utant
E ats everything
N aughty
A ngry
C reature
E normous.

Alfie Viner (8)
Our Lady Of The Assumption Primary School, Belle Vale

Adventure Time

Loko and his friends playing in the park
Always feeling bright, never feeling down
Lola falling down, Loko picks her up.
In Monsterville, with Loko and his friends,
On an adventure, always having fun.
Let's have an adventure with Loko and his friends.
We're going on a hut hunt to find a new house.
"Come with us and have some fun."

Edwina Attim (9)
South Norwood Primary School, South Norwood

Upside-Down Day

I was walking to school with a bored face
Until I saw a goofy, green-furred-looking thing but it seemed to look away
Very fast, but the same green-looking figure ran in front of me, but I
Couldn't stop in time.
The next thing I
Knew, it was me and the thing stumbling together on the floor. I was so late,
I couldn't catch up with my mate
And when I finally got to school, I forgot the date.
My teacher asked me, "Why are you late?"
The day started with maths.
We had a maths test.
I studied but I forgot everything
Because of the incident that happened this morning.
Last period was PE, we are learning cricket.
Our cricket coaches are called Dom and Basit.
But sadly,
When we got changed and everything, the teacher sadly

Told us that they caught the flu.
So we did some reading
But some of the reading
Books from our bookshelf were missing.
When I was going home, it appeared to me *again!*
But singing like a maniac
And I was cracking up
By the end.

Eldana Liewi (9)
St Anne's And Guardian Angels Catholic Primary School, London

Bowser The Smart Monster

On the way to Legoland, I saw a monster all
Sad and blue.
He was a dime, but he wasn't mine.
His teeth were white,
I named him Bowser
So I could remember to buy loads of trousers.
He spoke to me with glee
And explained, "My letter world exploded and I am now stuck here
My family are waiting for me
But I'm nowhere near!"
"Cheer up, little guy,
I'll take you to a spelling bee
Close by!"
"Hooray!" Bowser shouted, it was a dream
Come true.
He went in the line
And he did shine.
He spelt all the words correctly,
Bowser was happy.
He got a first-place medal, it

Glistened so much.
He'd never won something
That shone.
It was time to say goodbye
But I had an idea in my mind.
"Can you come tomorrow at the same time?"
"That's fine,"
Said Bowser, "See you next time!"

Flora Afolabi (9)
St Anne's And Guardian Angels Catholic Primary School, London

Gerald The Monster

On the way to school, I saw a monster.
This monster was from the forest and was trying to kill my friend.
I ran away, but the monster caught up with me
He started liking me
We became very good friends
We played football together
I asked him his favourite food
He said, "An avocado."
I said, let's go to the shop
So, that's where we went
But when we got there, the monster was mad because the shop was shut
But we did not give up
On the way, he told me his name,
It's Gerald
The next shop was also shut.
He was so moody,
So we went to my house since he didn't have one

I let him come into my house.
He ran straight to my room and started to smash things
I needed to feed him...

Reggie Matthews (9)
St Anne's And Guardian Angels Catholic Primary School, London

Slay The Monster

I was on the way to school with
My Gucci backpack, of course.
I walked down the corridors and couldn't
Find my classroom door.
I am a good person, but when
Someone steals my crown, you ain't liking
Me.
I usually eat caviar for my dinner
But now I'm into gold steak (with real gold
Of course!)
I'm about 3 foot 2 (I know, kind of
Small)
I woke up in the night, once
Looking at my feet, knowing I was too
Big for my bed.
I ran downstairs, jumping around
But then I realised I was just dreaming.
I was crying all night, I was really
So sad

And, by the way, I'm really 2 foot 2!
When I heard that, I cried even more
It was the worst day *ever!*

Isla Goodchild (8)
St Anne's And Guardian Angels Catholic Primary School, London

Grace

I was on my way to school with my sister who acted like a fool.
When I went in class, out of nowhere there was a blast
All my monster friends went to get an autograph and some wanted a photograph.
I was going home when I realised that I forgot my phone, I was as angry as a volcano.
I had to go back to school and I felt like a fool
And said, "Silly, slimy sausages," because I was surrounded by lots of monsters.
My bird nerd sister had to save me from those fans.
The next day was the holiday
So, me and my sister chose to go sky-diving.
What is fluffy? What is white? What can you see when skies are bright?
What can float? What brings rain? What may be higher than a bird or plane?

Zael Rose-Achiampong (9)
St Anne's And Guardian Angels Catholic Primary School, London

Monster Morning!

He crawled through the doggy door
Then landed on the floor!
He squeaked and squeaked and I became naive
As I quietly asked him to leave.
My mum asked why I was whispering
While my cat twitched his whiskers,
He ran up the stairs to my bedroom, and when he started to fuse
With the power, I got so confused!

As I walked to school that day
I never realised he came!
He was the size of a pom-pom
So he was disguised.
My friends, they tried to scare me by yelling out, "*Surprise!*"
I hid the little fur ball as he said goodbye
That was the last he saw of the school playground
That day.

Ruby Ader-Wrightson (9)
St Anne's And Guardian Angels Catholic Primary School, London

Octo-Rock

On the way to school,
I realised something
A new student was coming too!
Then, in my mind, came a ping!
Friendship bracelets!
But then I noticed,
Something was different
This student was naked
But he had scales
To cover his privates!
Oh, what a day
At school, we played and played

We went on an adventure together
Trying to find Fartland.
But there's an obstacle
In our way.
We have to try and do the fart
Code to enter.
We try and try again,

And we succeed, we
Farted and farted again and again.
I hope we do it again one day!

Maisha Delannoy (8)
St Anne's And Guardian Angels Catholic Primary School, London

Plane Time!

My Fizzy was lying on his sofa

Eating lots of candy and thinking
About going to the airport

And sneaking onto a flight
And going to Candy Land.

He got a suitcase and put all
Of his favourite things inside

And ran and ran and ran until
He got to the airport.

Next, he had to sneak past
Security.

After that, he got on a plane
And, finally, he got to
Candy Land!

Eliana Tekel (9)
St Anne's And Guardian Angels Catholic Primary School, London

Legoland Is A Dream

I was born in Fluffy Land and I
Moved to England to see my best friend.
We went to Legoland
When we got there, we forgot
Our fluffy tickets.
We've always wanted to go to
Legoland
Now Sandy and I were sad.
But I had an idea!
So, we snuck in and stayed all day
Then we went home
And we ate snacks
Until I had to pack
To go back
To Fluffy Land.

Stella Leiva Ospina (9)
St Anne's And Guardian Angels Catholic Primary School, London

The Monster

Monsters are big,
Monsters are small,
Monsters stink like a toilet bowl.
Monsters green,
Monsters are red,
Monsters have a stinky head.
The monsters went to school
And they used me as a tool.

Olivia Darby (8)
St Anne's And Guardian Angels Catholic Primary School, London

Monster Poetry - Creature Features

Harry And Me

My fuzzy, furry and friendly friend came from Mars to Earth...
Cute, cuddly and cat-like.
He stared like an owl to everyone nearby.
Each time he looked, he made a sound like 'earby!'

About a minute ago, I saw him.
I remembered him and I took him home.
We had many big, best adventures and we went to a volcano.
It was as big as Big Ben.

We were brave and went back home together.
One day, we went for a hike on Mount Everest, clumsy, exhausted and as excited as ever.
The mountain is rough, rocky and rotted.
Mount Everest is as big as a blue whale.

We were too cold, our skin went pale.
Once at the top, there was a big view.
We went for ages, our eyes drooped and dropped as we went back down.
We went back down and were as happy as a newborn puppy.

Luke Wong (8)
St Charles Borromeo Catholic Primary School, Weybridge

The Monster That Loves Ice Cream

Pinkie-pie is a funny, fun, fizzy, fuzzy monster.
Pinkie-pie is a funny, fun, fizzy, fuzzy, fluffy monster.
She loves ice cream a lot, she eats it for breakfast, lunch and dinner.
And every time she eats it, she feels like a winner.

Pinkie-pie is a funny, fun, fizzy, fuzzy, fluffy monster.
Pinkie-pie is a funny, fun, fizzy, fuzzy, fluffy-but-sweet-toothed monster.
Her favourite flavour is chocolate and she's beautiful like a baby owl.
She turns from pink to patchy brown and one day she screamed, "*Owwwwww!*"

Pinkie-pie is a funny, fun, fizzy, fuzzy, fluffy monster.
Pinkie-pie is a funny, fun, fizzy, fuzzy, fluffy, cute monster.
The ice cream that she loved had given Pinkie-pie some pain.

And when seeing the dentist, he said, "You're never to eat ice cream again."

Pinkie-pie is a funny, fun, fizzy, fuzzy, fluffy monster.
Pinkie-pie is a funny, fun, fizzy, fuzzy, fluffy-but-now-sad monster.
Walking home, the sobs of crying, missing her chocolate dream.
She met a girl, Breah, with a cone of, "*That's my ice cream!*"

Pinkie-pie is a funny, fun, fizzy, fuzzy, fluffy monster.
Pinkie-pie is a funny, fun, fizzy, fuzzy, wide-eyed monster.
"Oh, I'm sorry, I do like ice cream. It's the best and it's *soooo* nice," Breah giggled
"Oh yes, I agree, but you must brush every day, twice."
Pinkie-pie is a funny, fun, fizzy, fuzzy, fluffy, tooth-flossing monster
With a pop to a shop, basket with floss, brush and paste
She brushed, flossed and smiled in the mirror, knowing she's going to taste

Pinkie-pie is a funny, fun, fizzy, fuzzy, fluffy monster
Pinkie-pie is a funny, fun, fizzy, fuzzy, fluffy, happy monster
With the biggest smile ever, showing her all pearly whites
Chocolate ice cream is forever, it will always be Pinky-pie's.

Breah Rough (8)
St Charles Borromeo Catholic Primary School, Weybridge

Fluffball

My cool, crazy, cat-like creature went to Catland one day,
She was soft, small and silly, she loved to run and play.
She was as cute as a newborn kitten, wherever she went she left fur,
She would either hiss or miaow - she would never purr.

One day her funny, fuzzy friends took an angry tone,
They got awfully annoyed with her and left her all alone.
She was as lonely as an orphan, she was really sad,
Her friends were extremely mad!

Then she had an incredible, inspiring idea, she worked all day and night.
She was seriously sweaty and her tights were tight.
She made something as cute as herself - it was an adorable 'sorry' cat card.
Her friends were delighted because she had worked so hard.

Chloe Greenrod (8)
St Charles Borromeo Catholic Primary School, Weybridge

Meme The Monster

Meme is a monster, a mucky, messy monster
Have you heard of a 'Squidoctus'? 'Cause that is what she is.
Her father was an octopus, her mother was a squid,
Her sister was annoying and copied everything she did.

Today was Meme's first day at school and shy she was indeed,
She worried she'd be too different, according to her breed.
Meme picked up her backpack and stuffed a book inside
(If she didn't make any friends, this book is where she'd hide).

But by the end of her first day, she had so many friends,
Everyone was different - that seemed to be the trend!

Her favourite friend was 'Slimey' - like a ball of oopy gloop,
Who covered everyone in slime - it really was a hoot.

So if *you're* ever worried about trying something new,
Or making brand-new friends, now you'll know what to do.
Remember to just be yourself in everything you do,
You can be just like Meme - remember, she was different too.

Amelie Brown (8)
St Charles Borromeo Catholic Primary School, Weybridge

Spikey Strikes Again

Deep, deep down in the universe, there was a planet,
Not just a proper planet
But a world as strange as a crazy bunny,
With even stranger people, except, of course, for me.
Because, quite simply,
I am not strange at all.
The universe was at war with Mars,
And I went to Mars to get rid of the horrible aliens who were living there.
Spikey is one of the soldiers,
He picked up a pickled pepper sandwich from his bag.
He was crazy, clumsy and chattery.
And as creepy as a ghost.
It took a while to go all those miles,
When we got there, all we saw was dust, dust and dust.
And a bit later, aliens, aliens and aliens.
It was as tense as a Champions League final.
We were ready to invade.

The idea to invade finally started to work,
Even though the aliens were fighting back.
It was terribly tiring but, eventually, none of them were left.
We were as happy as children on a Christmas morning
And we flew back to our universe.

Luca Fumagalli (7)
St Charles Borromeo Catholic Primary School, Weybridge

The Cute And Creepy Cat

My cat-like, cute, cool friend came from a mysterious undiscovered universe...
My colourful, curious friend says her world is so much fun!
Everything in her universe is full of cat-like monsters...
Even a cat face for the sun!

Every time she tries to make a friend,
The magical power turns her into a scary cat monster!
And the 'friend' runs away...
At least she has me as a friend anyway.

One night, my monster - it's called Cutie - said,
"I am going to make another friend no matter what!"
So two of us travelled like an explorer an awful lot.
After four hours, we met a fluffy, furry dog monster friend.

"Woof! Woof!" (Hi, nice to meet you!)
"Meow! Meow!" (Hi, nice to meet you!)
Surprisingly, Dog Monster was not scared of Cutie at all!
Dog Monster and Cutie said, "Let's rock and roll!"

Ruby Lee (8)
St Charles Borromeo Catholic Primary School, Weybridge

Ruby's Adventure

My cute, casual and cuddly monster came from space...
She was as cute as a cat
When I saw her, I started to cartwheel all over the place!
But tomorrow is going to be fun because I'm bringing her to school.
The next day, my adorable, adventurous and amazing monster came to school, All the other children thought she was cool.
But I told them to be quiet because if the teachers knew, I would be in trouble.
Attending lunch,
My red panda-like monster ate all of my lunch
And then I had to get a new one.
But then it was time for class
And Ruby stayed hidden and quiet the whole time
So, when it was home time, I gave her a triple chocolate chip cookie
With a little ice cream on the side.

Kitty Macdougall (7)
St Charles Borromeo Catholic Primary School, Weybridge

The Heinous Crime And The Mighty Monster

My monster is fierce, fiery, and free,
She's also a bit clumsy, you'll see.
She once was small, like a little pine,
But then she witnessed a heinous crime.

She was scared, but didn't despair,
She summoned her power with a flare.
She made some fruit go sour and bad,
And the criminal never saw her pad.

A big pine tree fell on the bad guy,
As he screamed and shouted with a sigh.
"I taste sour fruit!" he cried and wept,
And my monster just sat there, well-slept.

I fed her cabbage that made her wild,
And soon she became a savage child.
But she saved the world with her might,
She went to sea and stole a pearl that shone bright.

Cassandra Pollicar (8)
St Charles Borromeo Catholic Primary School, Weybridge

My Monster

Once, I found a monster. He was slimy, smelly and slobbery.
He was green, grizzly and gross, but I gave him a strawberry,
I thought he liked me, but he didn't like me.
So, I said, "I really like you, why can't you see?"

When he met other people, they called him big, bad and boring.
I played some silly, stylish, stunning music, but he did not care to sing.
He is as big as a tree.
I don't think he can see or hear me.

I started to cry in a hard, heavily heartbroken way,
But then an amazing, astonishing thing, he said, "Can you play?"
He threw me up so high in the sky, I thought I could fly.
It was the best day, so I asked him to stay.

Daisy Cooper (8)
St Charles Borromeo Catholic Primary School, Weybridge

Monster Poetry - Creature Features

Lizzy Saves The World

Lizzy was sleeping in her bed peacefully
Until she heard slime-like sounds on the roof.
So, Lizzy went out of bed and looked out of the window
And she was terrified.
And, after that, she put on a cape and a superhero mask
And opened the window, flew out.
Swoosh!
She was trying to save the world from a slime
A slime was a slimy, toxic and hazardous creature
If you touched it...
Ummm...
Let's say you'd be ashes
Anyways, Lizzy's power is lightning
So then she used her lightning power on the slime.
And then the slime was defeated.
Boom!
A news reporter caught it on camera
And then everyone praised her for saving them.

Melissa Vacarro (8)
St Charles Borromeo Catholic Primary School, Weybridge

Orange

My monster is fizzy, friendly and funny.
Little, lucky and lazy.
My monster was as little as a slug.
And then finally ate breakfast.

He went to the park, playing alone.
His grandma and grandpa came to buy him a gift.
The gift was big as Orange.
And the gift was a statue of him.

His parent put the statue in his room.
Then he asked his grandma and grandpa how old they were.
They were like as old as seventy-five.
Orange is only six.

He has a great time eating lunch with his grandma and grandpa.
Grandma and Grandpa also buy a dog named Tabby.
Tabby was as little as a beetle.
Orange and his parents went to a shop to buy some dog food.

Colin Wong (8)
St Charles Borromeo Catholic Primary School, Weybridge

Monster Poetry - Creature Features

My Football-Loving Friend

My famous, fantastic, football friend came down in a rocket...
Handsome, hairy and helpful, so small he fits in my pocket!
As funny as a clown, he makes everybody laugh,
He is also smelly and really needs a bath!

Troublesome, terrific and teeny, he really can jump,
Green, gruesome and great, he loves a fist pump.
As green as a pea, he loves to take a shot,
Scoring with his head and feet, he really scores a lot.

Speedy, slimy and skilful, no one loves him more
Awesome, acrobatic and amazing, we really do adore
As quick as a cheetah, he runs on all fours
When he has the ball, he has magic at his feet and scores, scores, scores.

Sebastian Gibson (8)
St Charles Borromeo Catholic Primary School, Weybridge

My Monster Poem

My strong, scary, slimy, shivering monster woke up
And stepped out of his creepy, cool cave
He tripped on a wire and fell as hard as a rock
Into a trap full of boa constrictors

Out of nowhere, angry arrows started to fall around him
My brave, big, bold monster reacted in the blink of an eye
As quick as Usain Bolt he started to shoot back
Suddenly he fell asleep as the poisoned dart started to work

My deadly, dangerous, daring monster opened his eyes
To find himself lying face-to-face with a ravenous, rotten rat
He screamed as loud as a baby but started to laugh
When he realised it had all been a bad dream!

Eli-James Frontado (8)
St Charles Borromeo Catholic Primary School, Weybridge

Monster Poetry - Creature Features

My Rainbow Monster

My funny, friendly, fluffy monster comes from far away.
Cute, cuddly and colourful, she is here to stay.
As pretty as a rainbow, she holds me very tight,
Magically creating happy dreams for me all night.

My happy, hairy, hungry monster eats my bad dreams.
She is particularly clever, kind and caring, it seems.
As hungry as a caterpillar, she swallows them whole,
Instantly soothing and looking after my soul.

My cheery, chubby, chirpy monster is truly special,
Bulky, bubbly, bouncy and rather unusual.
As loyal as a dog, she's always by my side,
And with her around, there's no need to hide.

Alicia Barnea Choi (7)
St Charles Borromeo Catholic Primary School, Weybridge

When Ginger Ring Monster Goldy Came To Tea

My ginger ring monster Goldy is frizzy, fluffy, friendly and super.
He is a kind and loving monster who likes to play the PS4009F game.
He is as tall as a fuzzy giraffe,
When, at last, finally, Ginger Ring Monster met me in my house.

He was as tall and as super as a tiger on its feet,
It has claws as sharp as a knife.
My monster is as cuddly as a teddy bear
When we went out for tea and cake and to buy a teddy bear.

He is as excited as a dog fetching a ball
He is as friendly as a doctor
He is as tall as an adult
When, finally, we got to the café to fetch some tea.

Cian Wilson (8)
St Charles Borromeo Catholic Primary School, Weybridge

Monster Poetry - Creature Features

Slime The Monster

A dangerous, dismal, disgusting creature
His name is Slime the monster.
What a smelly, stinky, slimy, nasty feature.

As bouncy as a ball
He is slippery and tall
And with his four different eyes
He eats pies full of flies.

He scoffs and coughs,
He munches and crunches.
What a frightful sight to see him eat his tea,
You would never believe he's only age three.

At night
When there's no light
And he catches the moon, he turns bright green.

Peter Counsell (8)
St Charles Borromeo Catholic Primary School, Weybridge

How Two Monsters Became Friends

The green, great Geoffrey.
A monster who had long, leafy limbs.
He was as green as freshly cut grass.
One evening, he saw a monster in the distance.

The super, strong Sam.
In a big, buzzing buggy.
The buggy was as red as a beetroot.
And they walked closer together and became friends.

They played a fun, friendly football game.
They were lucky that it didn't rain.
It was as fun as a waterpark.
In the end, they drew the game and became best friends.

Edmund Santamaria (8)
St Charles Borromeo Catholic Primary School, Weybridge

Roasted Monster

Roasted Monster, Roasted Monster!

He was playing on a tyre with his friend, Maya.
He got stopped by the choir singing 'Harry Maguire...'
But refused to join 'cause of his stammer...
Even though he was a good drummer.
Oh, what a clumsy 'liar'.

Roasted Monster, Roasted Monster

He played with Maya until he could not tire.
But met bad Mariah who tripped him on a wire...
And he fell in a fire.

Oh, *Roasted Monster!*

Christian Muzengi (7)
St Charles Borromeo Catholic Primary School, Weybridge

Monster Fin

Slimy, slim, silly monster, Fin
With green, greyish, golden skin
As smelly as a pile of stinky socks,
He hides behind trees and rocks

Friendly, funny monster, Fin,
Makes a dreary, dreadful din,
As noisy as a howling hound,
Everyone can hear his sound.

Lucky, loveable monster, Fin
With a great, glad, glowing grin
He's as funny as a silly clown,
He can make a smile from any frown.

Jonas Baptista (7)
St Charles Borromeo Catholic Primary School, Weybridge

My Crazy, Cool Monster

My crazy, cool monster
Came from Planet Drool
His body was inflated
And he loved to keep up to date

His name is Darwin
And he is very red
If you take a peek at him
Then your mind will fill with dread

His hobby
Is running inside
Because it is slippery
So he gets a lot of injuries

So now you know
About my
Crazy, cool monster
How about you find your own?

Oliver Wever (8)
St Charles Borromeo Catholic Primary School, Weybridge

Groot Landed On Earth

Groot just landed on Planet Earth.
(He smells like a trashcan).
He came to collect me, we were going to Groot's house on Mars.

Once we landed, there were baddies trying to capture us
So, we went and fought them (we won).
"Hooray," we said, then we kept going.

We're lucky we find more friends to help us.

Benjamin Wright (8)
St Charles Borromeo Catholic Primary School, Weybridge

The Big Fat Chilli

My monster is called the Big Fat Chilli
And in the morning I take him on a walk every day.
He is a happy monster
Because he loves going for exciting walks all the day
And when he gets to his lovely hotel.
Then, in the afternoon,
He loves to roll around in his fantastic bed.
And then he goes to bed
For five hours.

William Sifton (8)
St Charles Borromeo Catholic Primary School, Weybridge

Fuzzy-Roy Can Help The Earth

My monster is clumsy, cute and clean.
My monster is silly, smart and shy.
My monster is as smooth as a spoon.
Then my monster helped the Earth, just like me.
And I wondered, *is he smart and shy like me?*
Or is he not smart and shy like me?

Avery Gibson (7)
St Charles Borromeo Catholic Primary School, Weybridge

The Lonely Dragon

The dragon's moans filled the sky, in a high-pitched scream
Down below, hundreds of archers fired arrows into the screaming dragon
It had only meant to find food for its egg and now was riddled with arrows
She gave a last blood-curdling scream and died.
The soldiers gave a cheer of, "Hooray," but then it happened.
Chip, chip, chip, the egg broke,
The new dragon roared with the intensity of a thousand suns,
And breathed a tongue of fire that burned the wood to a crisp
And he left no survivors.

Mannix Grant (9)
Surlingham Community Primary School, Surlingham

My Monster

This monster can be vicious,
And also sometimes kind,
But whatever it does,
It always uses its mind.

This monster does drink,
It seems to be drinking blood,
It drinks quite a lot,
But it doesn't ever cause a blood flood

His teeth are like vampire's
They are very sharp
They can bite through anything
From metal to a carp.
He has quite a lot of fur,
Coloured black and red

When he meets another monster,
He hits them with his head.

His arms are leaves
Coloured red and green
In autumn, they fall off
Making everybody scream.

Freya Dunning (7)
Surlingham Community Primary School, Surlingham

Monsters Are Big, Monsters Are Small

Monsters are big, monsters are small.
Some are round, some are tall.

My monster, Fringe, has terrible hair
It's long and greasy and gets everywhere
But he's my monster, so I don't care.

He's fun to be with, he likes to be outside
Sometimes, we get on our bikes and go for a ride
One day, I'll take him to school
Everyone will love him because I think he's cool.

Hugo McKinney (8)
Surlingham Community Primary School, Surlingham

I Am Unique

I am Maddy
People think I'm scary
I am not
And I'm certainly not hairy.

I am unique
As slimy as can be
I am a shape-shifter
You can't catch me.

I came from Pluto
Until it was no more
Now on Earth
I may be at your door.

I may seem scary
I think I'm a little cute
Would you like to be friends?
I can be a hoot.

Penny Gregory (9)
Surlingham Community Primary School, Surlingham

Glob

A glob, a glob,
It does nothing at all,
Until it starts to drool.

A glob, a glob,
It sits like a slob,
It all goes wrong,
When it starts to pong.

A glob, a glob,
A poor, lonely glob,
It can't do much,
Until it can clutch and touch.

A glob, a glob,
With that touch, he mends,
For now, he can play with his friends.

Oliver Lincoln (8)
Surlingham Community Primary School, Surlingham

My Monster

My monster is called Terry
He is very merry
His arms are flippers
On his feet are slippers
His square body is red
And he has three eyes on his head
He is very kind
And he has a good mind
He has many nice buddies
And in his spare time, he loves studies
He enjoys wearing his spotty bowtie
But he really wishes he could fly.

Toby S (9)
Surlingham Community Primary School, Surlingham

Nally

Nally's shy and scared of humans
Especially loud, noisy hooligans.
Nally's green
But he's not lean.
You may think he's dangerous
But he's harmless.
He comes from Planet Neelo
His only friend is Lelo.
Nally's really furry
His fur is curly.
People hunt him in his cave
Nally just needs to be brave.

Izaac Fisher (8)
Surlingham Community Primary School, Surlingham

What You Overlook

There are many things you overlook
That hide in crannies, cracks and little nooks
Many creatures lurk or learn
That you foolishly overlook and should your head turn,
You will not want them to learn
All those things you overlook
That hide in crannies, cracks and nooks
This last bit you won't like
They will find a moment to strike.

Oran Grant (9)
Surlingham Community Primary School, Surlingham

The Good Monster

He's good, not bad,
His name is Funny,
And he's as fluffy as
A cuddly bunny.

Funny is excited and
Really quite happy,
So much that his ears
Went all flappy.

He went on a roller coaster
Which was really very bumpy
So very bumpy that
Funny got jumpy.

Ella Hambling (8)
Surlingham Community Primary School, Surlingham

Monster Chap

It lives under caves
It's not what it says
It's hairy
But it's not scary
It can fly
It can spy with its five eyes
It is vegetarian
But it's not pescetarian
It goes to school
But it can't play football
It has stitches
It can't eat Twizzlers.

Lee Codling (8)
Surlingham Community Primary School, Surlingham

Gerbil The Monster

This is a monster from the planet Slerp
And this is where he likes to lurk
In cold, damp places
Hiding in small spaces
He has a very kind heart
But horrible faces
Everyone is scared, but really he is kind
And that is what he wants everyone to find.

Sadie Rae (9)
Surlingham Community Primary School, Surlingham

Monster

Monsters wiggle and wriggle.
They smell like trash, so they should get thrashed.
They are furry, slimy and naughty.
And, I should add, they're not really awesome
Now, what do you think flying, shape-shifter and snake-like monsters are like?

Arthur Hall (8)
Surlingham Community Primary School, Surlingham

My Special Monster

Once upon a time, when I was six,
I went shopping to buy a Twix.
I caused my mum a huge delay,
Because I got lost along the way.
I found myself in a deep, dark cave,
And tried my best to be brave,
I kept thinking of my mum and teacher,
Oh, no! There is a creature
It was big, purple with pink spots
And had massive black eyes like dots
I looked at it and said hello,
It smiled and said, "Hey, bro."
It had long hairy arms like snakes
With horrible dry skin covered in flakes
The creature waved its arms around
Without making any sound.
I was so scared, I began to cry,
I was so sure I was going to die.
The monster smiled and looked at me
I thought, *where can I flee?*
He said, "Do you want to see my best tricks?"

Before I answered, he pulled out a Twix
We ate it together and became friends
This is where the story ends.

Libby Howell (7)
Ysgol Carreg Hirfaen, Cwmann

The Fynnky Land

I'm from The Fynnky Land
My name is Bobita

      S mall and big too
      M onster Land bad, Fynnky Land the best
      A lso, Fynnky Land is the best place for holidays
      L avender is my favourite colour
      L ove Monster Land and come to Fynnky Land

      B ecause Fynnky Land is so much better
yo **U** have to come to Fynnky Land.
      T omorrow, I, Bobita, am going to the playground

      "**I** 'm going to the playground," said I, Bobita
      M ost fun comes from Fynnky Land.

      B obita, I, love pizza
      I dislike spiders, but likely there are no spiders in Fynnky Land
      G ot to go to the party tonight.

Monster Poetry - Creature Features

G o to the party, Bobita," said my friend.
E nter Fynnky Land and your life will change with fun and excitement
R oads made out of candy and biscuits.

Tirion Tomos (11)
Ysgol Carreg Hirfaen, Cwmann

Snowy The Monster

Once upon a time, when I was eight,
I was playing in the park and it was great.
All my friends were there, having fun,
It was lovely being out in the sun.

All of a sudden, the clouds went black
And from the bushes I heard a great crack.
I went over to have a look
What I saw was no fairy, it was very scary.

It was a monster with light purple skin
It also had wings, but they were very thin.
Bright yellow stripes covered its back
And cute baby eyes that were black.

All of a sudden, I heard the ice cream van sound
And completely forgot what I had just found
I wanted an ice cream covered in honey
But in my pocket was no money.

The monster smiled and said, "Get one for me,
We will eat it together under the tree."
He gave me some coins, I went to the van
That's how our friendship began.

Emelia Howell (8)
Ysgol Carreg Hirfaen, Cwmann

Atalia

A talia is mysterious because she's always blending
T alons disappear whilst wings appear.
A mazing every time she flies
L and! At last! We've been flying for hours
I s it Atalia? That girl acts like her!
A lleys we pass as we fly through the city.

T he ground is shaking as Atalia the giant wakes up
H ello! Is that you, Atalia?! Where are you?
E verything is blue when Atalia goes

M onsters are all different with their powers.
O nline - Atalia is always online now since Covid.
N ow everything is blooming again, everyone is different
S cales are here as Atalia is suddenly a mermaid
T ails and two mahogany claws appear
E very day, Atalia is in a different form
R ed eyes look up as Atalia finally is herself.

Lilybet Cousinne (10)
Ysgol Carreg Hirfaen, Cwmann

Monster Poetry - Creature Features

The Shape-Shifting Dragon

As I walked through the forest, I stopped and saw
A very rough body and many, many claws.
I shouted and screamed and climbed over crumbling rocks.
At the top was a castle with many fine locks.
It was a long, strong castle and it gave me hope
So, I shouted and pleaded and they let down a rope.
As I climbed up the rope, whose feet did I see?
Only a monster's, looking down at me.
Cruel, clawed feet, yellow eyes and a sharp horn
The dragon had got me, all my hopes were torn
Suddenly, the dragon transformed into a girl
Red hair, green eyes and a crown filled with pearls
She smiled and she said, "Don't be so sad,
I'm the shape-shifting dragon and I'm really not bad."

Oleanna Cousinne (8)
Ysgol Carreg Hirfaen, Cwmann

Bonnie The Monster

B onnie is a fluffy monster.
O fferloffergusly is where he lies.
N o one really knows him very well.
N ormally, Bonnie is very well-behaved.
I know he loves cuddles.
E ven his friends think he is funny. Thousands of monsters live in Offerloffergusly. Everyone thinks Bonnie is flexible.

M um and Dad call him Squish Mallow.
O nly Bonnie knows how to look after kids.
N ever hurt his fuzzy, warm heart.
S elling his scrumptious soup.
T alented, tall Dad fixes cars
E agle-eyed Mum is a photographer.
R esponsible Bonnie looks after children, caring.

Poppy Griffiths (11)
Ysgol Carreg Hirfaen, Cwmann

Monster Monty

M onty likes the rainforest. He slithers all day long. He likes the pythons, but the pythons don't like Monty.
O n sunny days, he hides in his den, he hopes he doesn't find the jaguar or that the jaguar finds him!
N o one helps him because he's very slimy and has fangs. He likes humans for lunch!
S omeone's hiding in the shadows, who could it be? It was the python, fighting the jaguar!
T he night is quiet. Everybody is quiet. Monty had a nightmare about a wildfire.
E asily battling the wildfire with all his strength, he blew it out with all his might!
R elieved that he saved the rainforest.

Jessica Burtenshaw-Jones (7)
Ysgol Carreg Hirfaen, Cwmann

Wilow The Monster

W ilow the monster
"I am Wilow," that's all she says
L ots of light flashing around her ear
O oh, she looks so peculiar
W ith a triangle head and a square body

T he skipping-with-one-leg expert
H er house is enormous, but no family
E ar that spins around like a windmill

M illy is her friend
O oh, she is so lively
N o one is more fluffy than her
S he is so kind
T elling jokes like a clown
E xpert at an Easter egg hunt
R elaxed and laidback, the one and only Wilow!

Esther Jones (9)
Ysgol Carreg Hirfaen, Cwmann

Monster Poetry - Creature Features

Dancing Monster - Do Not Be Fooled!

D ancing Dolly dances all night.
A lways fooling her victims coming too close
N ot suspicious of Dancing Dolly's hair.
C utting-edge timing has Dolly got.
I ntelligently drawing in her prey while dancing all the time.
N earer and nearer come her prey.
"G ot you!" she shouts as her victim is strangled.

D oing her process again and again.
O ut she goes to the disco every night.
L ights of the disco make Dolly sparkle.
L ifting her dress, twirling and dancing.
Y ou should take care when Dolly is near!

Mair Hopkins (11)
Ysgol Carreg Hirfaen, Cwmann

Jay The Monster

My monster's name is Jay, he's got five eyes
He's got hair everywhere
His friends are Jim and Bob
He's got wings like a kite
And a tongue like a snake
He is from England
He is very, very tall.

He was going to the movies and then he went to sit down
And then Bob and Jim said, "You're on the screen,"
And Jay said, "Oh, that was the film I videoed last night
And it's called 'My name is Jay and these
Are my friends, Bob and Jim'.

Bob was very happy
And Jim was very happy too
So, they went back home in a good mood.

Tom Hari (10)
Ysgol Carreg Hirfaen, Cwmann

Monster Poetry - Creature Features

Rubber Monster

Rubber ducky, Rubber Monster
They both clean everywhere
They are best friends
One is on the top half of the world
And the other is on the other side.
Once, when they cleaned a kitchen
They got stained by a bottle of food colouring
They got a *red spot!*
They didn't look the same
So, they licked and licked and licked but it didn't work
So, they went to the shop but they couldn't open the food colouring
It fell and spilled over the floor
And jumped but they weren't in the right spot
So, they stayed different.

Lisa Adcock Williams (8)
Ysgol Carreg Hirfaen, Cwmann

America's Monster

I went to America, took a trip, with my family.
We went on a walk using a map,
A map that took us into the woods.
We were playing in the park and there was a monster creeping up,
Creeping up from behind a tree.
He was tall, hairy and scary,
So scary we felt like we wanted to run.
Stomping loudly and laughing delightedly,
He walked to us, walked slowly like a turtle.
All three of us ran straight back to the hotel,
The hotel door was locked.
That same night we flew home,
Home and safe from America's monster.

Jacob Hall (8)
Ysgol Carreg Hirfaen, Cwmann

Monster Poetry - Creature Features

Popsi Says

Hi, my name is Popsi
I'm from the Positive planet
I'm a fluffy, kind and happy monster
I love to help children feel better
So, if you are feeling sad, anxious or
Worried or just need a hug
I'll fly down from the sky
At 2 million miles per hour
I'll zoom around the world
To find you!
And when I do...
I'll give *you*...
The loveliest, warmest, biggest
Hug and squeeze
So you'll never be alone with me
And don't forget, *don't worry.*

Chloe Ling (10)
Ysgol Carreg Hirfaen, Cwmann

Run, Monster, Run

Run, red monster
As fast as you can
I'm coming after you
With my Ghostbuster gun
No, I like you, monster
Don't run away
I want to watch football
In the big stadium
Do you want to play football with me?
I love it so much
I'm sure you will too
I support Liverpool
And my favourite player is Mo Salah
We can all play together
And be the best of friends
Because you are a friendly monster
Who is your favourite player?
I hope it's me, my friend.

Benjamin Davies (7)
Ysgol Carreg Hirfaen, Cwmann

Monster Poetry - Creature Features

That's My Friend, Spike

You wouldn't like a fight with my friend, Spike,
He is very strong and has a powerful bite

You wouldn't like to eat with my friend, Spike,
He is very hangry and eats everything in his sight

You wouldn't like to do football with my friend, Spike,
He'll toss and turn and his breath might burn

You wouldn't like to fly with my friend, Spike,
He is faster than the speed of light and would probably give you a fright.

That's my friend, Spike.

Ifan Jones (10)
Ysgol Carreg Hirfaen, Cwmann

Timmy The Monster

Timmy's a monster,
He lives in our house,
He's sometimes quite scary,
His favourite food is mouse.

He is black and white,
His eyes are shiny and bright,
He has a tail like a snake,
Every night, he keeps me awake.

He howls and he yowls,
He scratches and scrapes,
He chases me around,
There is no escape!

He lies down on a chair,
He really doesn't care.
His tail wraps around him in a bend.
He really is my best friend!

Alis Jones (11)
Ysgol Carreg Hirfaen, Cwmann

There Was A Monster At School

There was a monster at school
He was big, green and blue
He was a little bit smelly
And 12ft 2.

He had three pink eyes,
Tiny arms like French fries,
A big wobbly belly
And an angry face like Aunt Nelly.

He made a terrible noise!
It shook all of the toys
Poor Mrs Mabel
She was hiding under the table.

There was a monster at school
But I wasn't afraid.
I just held his tiny hand
Then we went out and played.

Cerys Jones (11)
Ysgol Carreg Hirfaen, Cwmann

Fruit Buster

B lob Berry lands in his fruit mobile
L eaving Planet Passion Fruit for his mission
O n Planet Earth with fruitastic tricks
B oys and girls are curious to see

B ananas, blueberries, blackberries bouncing down the street
E veryone wondering, what's going on?
R oads closed, streets are full, Blob is throwing fruit around
R un and get your five a day
Y ou know you need it anyway!

Llio Richards (11)
Ysgol Carreg Hirfaen, Cwmann

Scared

Scared, I wish I could get out of this room.
My body is full of gloom.
If anybody finds me, I'll be so happy.
But no one's gonna do that, not even a bat.
This monster is right by me.
So, I'm under the spare mat.
Scared... now yay! I'm out of this room
And so the monster is too.
I'm practising to fight in a wrestling ring.
The monster goes to a bad bat cave.
If you want to know, my name is Dave!

Callum Gale (8)
Ysgol Carreg Hirfaen, Cwmann

My Little Monster

My little monster, as cute as can be,
Likes to play with his friends Timmy and Bee
They play in the park all day
And have a lot of fun when they hide away
He meets more people to fill his day with joy
They all play together and he's enjoyed
He comes home all lonely and sad
But remembers all the plans tomorrow has
He gets tucked away in bed and starts to dream
He thinks, *what an adventure today has been.*

Elin Dafydd Lewis (11)
Ysgol Carreg Hirfaen, Cwmann

Monster Poetry - Creature Features

Merry Little Blossom

B lossom loves her crackers on a Sunday afternoon
L oves her cat as well as that, his name is Billy Moon
O ddly enough, she has no legs, and she likes the rain
S he can float above the wet and over every drain.
S ometimes, she leaves the moon and floats right down to Wales.
O n Mondays and Thursdays, she likes to cuddle snails
M erry little Blossom is my favourite friend.

Menna Greasley (10)
Ysgol Carreg Hirfaen, Cwmann

The Cuddle Monster

I have a special friend that only I can see,
His name is The Cuddle Monster and he likes to play with me.
He is not scary or mean,
He is fun and likes to dream.
When I am feeling blue,
He knows just what to do.
He dreams up lots of games to play,
To keep me happy through the day.
Sometimes, I feel too many things, it gets me in a muddle,
So, what he does is stop the game to give me a big cuddle.

Theo Syrett-Bibby (9)
Ysgol Carreg Hirfaen, Cwmann

Stitch The Shape-Shifting Rabbit

S titch is a happy rabbit that can shape-shift.
T ime is one of the things Stitch can control!
I nside, on a rainy day, Stitch sometimes changes it to sunny weather!
T o a bad monster, Stitch will shape-shift into a weapon and fight him.
C ontrolling the weather is one of Stitch's favourite things
H aving powers makes Stitch tired sometimes because it uses a lot of energy.

Erica Burtenshaw-Jones (9)
Ysgol Carreg Hirfaen, Cwmann

Moaning's Meeting Story

Moaning was moaning about his money
His wallet was empty, which wasn't funny
He called his boss and asked for a meeting
Because he was cold and couldn't afford the heating
His boss said, "Moaning, that's quite a surprise,"
But he wasn't happy to give a pay rise
Moaning the monster said, "Listen to me,
If I don't get a pay rise, I'm going to flee."

Morgan Williams (8)
Ysgol Carreg Hirfaen, Cwmann

Monster Poetry - Creature Features

The Big Foot

My monster has large round eyes,
He has sharp, pointed teeth,
His mouth is dark and wide,
He has very slimy skin,
My monster doesn't have a nose,
His arms are long and thin,
He has legs like tree trunks,
His body is so big,
My monster lives in a dark, gloomy cave,
He eats slimy sea snails and slugs,
He walks with a big jump, and naps,
He has a very scary growl.

Ava-May Gregson (8)
Ysgol Carreg Hirfaen, Cwmann

Clawsome The Naughty Monster

Clawsome is a naughty monster
Who lives up in the trees
He likes to swing from every branch
That he sees.

Clawsome is a scary monster
But sweet and nice
He likes to prank his furry friends, but is super
Scared of mice.

Clawsome is a hairy monster
With big, brown, googly eyes
He likes to sit up in the trees
Scratching fleas.

Celyn Efa Jones (9)
Ysgol Carreg Hirfaen, Cwmann

The Monster

Once, I saw a monster,
It was so hairy.
When I got close,
It was really scary.
It had five eyes,
It was *big* and alive.
It liked to fly,
Up high in the sky.
It likes to eat,
Frogs and sweets.
With every bite,
It grows with might.
And then I blinked,
What did I see?
But one of those eyes,
Staring back at me!

Lili Jones (9)
Ysgol Carreg Hirfaen, Cwmann

My Monster, Lily

L ove is the best.
O range is the colour of my monster.
V ery kind is my monster.
I ndependent and can do things.
N aughty and happy.
G rowls a lot too.

L icks my face when she's excited
I maginary friend.
L ikes to sleep a lot.
Y ou are my favourite monster.

Poppy Scaife (8)
Ysgol Carreg Hirfaen, Cwmann

Sunny, The Monster At Home

My lovely little monster
She looks like a lobster.
Her favourite colour is pink
And she likes her drink.
She likes fruit
She does not like tying her boot.
She has a lovely colour green
She is not very mean.
She has patterns like a leaf
She likes eating beef.
Her claws are very sharp
But she has a loving heart.

Nia (8)
Ysgol Carreg Hirfaen, Cwmann

Terry In Africa

He starts with a 'T',
He's big,
He has a yellow stripe,
He is now older than the tyranno-lizard king T-rex,
He travelled to Africa,
On the back of a bike,
With two best friends, Spiny and Tank,
He and his friends arrived at a safari,
Met new friends,
The elephant herd,
The dominators of the land.

John Lewis (9)
Ysgol Carreg Hirfaen, Cwmann

My Friend, Vangi

My monster, Vangi, is kind and friendly,
My friends see him as scary
He is very hairy

He sleeps with me in my double bed
And he drinks my tea and eats my bread

He's small and rolls into a ball
To play football

He's sometimes naughty
But he's very sporty.

My friend, Vangi.

Sebastian Jac Gregson (9)
Ysgol Carreg Hirfaen, Cwmann

Monsters

When you think of monsters, you can get quite scared!
The fangs, the teeth, the hair and the way the eyes glare
But when you meet my monster, you don't need to be alarmed.
He's friendly, short and funny, and green from head to toe.
So, when you see my monster, don't hide or run away
Come and play today.

Mia Hargreaves (11)
Ysgol Carreg Hirfaen, Cwmann

Mischievous Millie

M onstrous
I ncredibly scary
L oving
L arge
I nfamous
E nergetic

T rouble
H orrible
E xciting

M agical
O ld
N otorious
S caly
T errifying
E xtreme
R ough.

Amelia Edwards (11)
Ysgol Carreg Hirfaen, Cwmann

The Bullseye

M onster Bullseye, as slimy as can be.
O n Planet Mars is where he can be seen.
N o monster is as deadly as Bullseye.
S pooky Bullseye loves Halloween.
T oenails like feral cat claws.
E normous Bullseye, as large as an elephant.
R emember to stay away from Bullseye.

Megan Thomas (11)
Ysgol Carreg Hirfaen, Cwmann

Friendly Monster

One cold evening,
I was sat by the window
Reading a book.

I saw something crawling
From under my bed
It had long black arms.
Fox-like ears.
Sharp, pointed teeth
And a colourful body.

I screamed with terror,
Only to discover it was
Fungus the friendly
Monster.

Amelia Rees (8)
Ysgol Carreg Hirfaen, Cwmann

Big Fluffy Monster

- **M** assive and brave
- **O** h no, please do not go near this monster
- **N** asty monster
- **S** ecret bunker in Australia, that's where he lives
- **T** he big, fluffy, scary monster is on the loose
- **E** normous monster coming to eat you
- **R** un, Gakpo will catch you.

Cai Davies (10)
Ysgol Carreg Hirfaen, Cwmann

Spikey Power

- **S** uper helpful orange monster
- **P** lanet Prickly is where he is from
- **I** nside he's warm and cuddly but outside all prickly
- **K** ind and caring with healing hands
- **E** yes so scary, big, round and black
- **Y** ellow teeth so strong and sharp but he has the greatest.

Brychan Richards (8)
Ysgol Carreg Hirfaen, Cwmann

My Monster

My monster is special to me
He never stops talking, you see
He lives in my basement
As friendly as can be
His favourite snack is crackers and cheese
Whenever I offer, he always says please
He sneaks through the woods late at night
And in the moonlight.

Joshua Davies (10)
Ysgol Carreg Hirfaen, Cwmann

Volvo

My monster's name is Volvo
He is from the Volvo dealership
In Swansea,
He makes cups of tea
For people in the Volvo dealership.
My monster is very well-behaved
If I were a monster
I would go to Japan
To drive the Hitachi diggers.

Henry Gillard (8)
Ysgol Carreg Hirfaen, Cwmann

Monster

- **M** y monster's name is Mike
- **O** ne massive eye he has
- **N** ice, kind and funny to all
- **S** hort like a tree stump
- **T** ries his hardest at football
- **E** veryone's best friend
- **R** espectful to everyone he meets.

Celt Davies (9)
Ysgol Carreg Hirfaen, Cwmann

Tod The Monster

M y little monster
O nly loves me
N obody knows that
S o lucky, lucky me
T he amount of time we spend together
E xplains why we're friends
R eally want Tod to be my friend forever and ever.

Jake Jones (10)
Ysgol Carreg Hirfaen, Cwmann

Jack Spike

He tricks you with one look,
Fools you with three books.
Can make you fight him,
But kills you first
Then eats you up,
Like a big cup.
He looks pretty,
But is actually *scary!*
Take care when Jack Spike is near.

Elin Hopkins (9)
Ysgol Carreg Hirfaen, Cwmann

Monster

M y monster is called Glwmi.
O n his body is light pink fur.
N ever naughty, but always
S cares me.
T otally jiggly when he walks.
E ats a lot of candy
R emember, it's only a dream!

Siwan Haf Davies (7)
Ysgol Carreg Hirfaen, Cwmann

My Monster

His name is Tim
Tilted Towers is his favourite game
His best friend is me, Gwion
He needs to keep his dig on
We walk for miles through
The woods
Going on big adventures
Where we will be the greatest
Inventors.

Gwion Howden (7)
Ysgol Carreg Hirfaen, Cwmann

Steve The Monster

Steve's got two eyes shining bright,
And fangs that give you quite a fright,
But behind that scary disguise,
Are floaty paws and cuddly thighs,
Approach with care and you might find,
A monster that's gentle and kind.

Cara Jones (9)
Ysgol Carreg Hirfaen, Cwmann

Bob The Monster

There once was a monster called Bob
With two friends called Jim and Jimmy,
They lived in Pumsaint Gold Mines.

They really wanted to go
To France and go
Up the Eiffel Tower
He's a good and fast monster.

Tomos Evans (10)
Ysgol Carreg Hirfaen, Cwmann

George The Skinny Monster!

He is a baby, naughty monster for Evie.
Scariest monster George is.
And he goes to the park every day.
George decides.
George.
And he is so scary George is.
And so fiery George is.
And very scary is George.

Evie Haf Williams (8)
Ysgol Carreg Hirfaen, Cwmann

Monsters

My monster's name is Mickey,
Open the door to see Mickey,
Now it's in the house somewhere,
Shh, I can hear Mickey the monster,
There he is!
"Ehh, you found me."
Ran Mickey the monster quickly.

Ellis Jones (9)
Ysgol Carreg Hirfaen, Cwmann

Chichen

C hichen is my name
H a, ha, I'm very funny
I can breathe fire
C hicken is my favourite food
H ome is in a cave
E arthworms are my friends
N ight-time is my day.

Aron Russell (8)
Ysgol Carreg Hirfaen, Cwmann

Bob The Blob

My name is Bob
I'm a bit of a slob
My skin is green
And I'm very mean
I'm incredibly rude
When I'm chewing my food
My breath is *soo* smelly
And my tummy wobbles like jelly.

Oliver Readwin (11)
Ysgol Carreg Hirfaen, Cwmann

Monsters

Monsters are big, monsters are small
My monster isn't very tall
Monsters are scary, some are cute
My monster plays the flute
Monsters are hairy, monsters are rough
My monster is full of fluff.

Eva Bevan (8)
Ysgol Carreg Hirfaen, Cwmann

James

J ames is a big scary monster
A fter a long time, James is lonely
M agical powers James has
E normous meals James gets
S hape-shifts with his magic and scares people off.

Rheinallt Davies (10)
Ysgol Carreg Hirfaen, Cwmann

Monster Island

It all began on Monster Island
Where there were 1000s of monsters
But one of the monsters looked scary
Mommy monster said, "Are you okay?"
Baby monster said, "Yes, I am fine."

Zoe Evans (8)
Ysgol Carreg Hirfaen, Cwmann

A Monster From Space

Monster, monster up in the sky
Monster, monster, come down and say hi
Monster, monster with your big scary eyes
Monster, monster with green slimy slime
Monster, monster, it is time to shine.

Leo Gale (8)
Ysgol Carreg Hirfaen, Cwmann

Pup Academy Monster

My monster is lovely and sweet
She runs down the street
The volcano is very hot
She gets tired a lot
I took her to the Pup Academy to make friends
Now she was in there to the end.

Evie Langford (7)
Ysgol Carreg Hirfaen, Cwmann

Billy

Rumbling, roaring tummy made
Children very scared and
He lives in a bin that looks like a big gherkin
And he is green like grass
He is as big as a three-year-old boy.

Gruff Pexton (7)
Ysgol Carreg Hirfaen, Cwmann

Scary Grimthorn

Grimthorn's big and scary
A sight to make you wary
But don't let his looks deceive
His fur is oh-so fluffy
Approach with caution or you'll be sorry.

Niamh Jones (9)
Ysgol Carreg Hirfaen, Cwmann

Jelly The Monster

J elly is amazing
E yes like yours are so pretty
L ove you, Jelly
L ive, laugh, love, Jelly
Y ou, Jelly, are my friend.

Cadi Fflur Davies (10)
Ysgol Carreg Hirfaen, Cwmann

Vecna The Killer

V ery dangerous and evil
E xtremely horrifying
C ausing death and destruction
N ever to be trusted
A lways keep away!

Cai Jones (8)
Ysgol Carreg Hirfaen, Cwmann

Monster Charlie

There was a monster called Charlie
He was very mean to other monsters
Charlie was a bully
Charlie called his brother
Out loud, with his voice.

Cadi Rowcliffe (8)
Ysgol Carreg Hirfaen, Cwmann

Monster Party

Dragon flew to the party
He was very farty!
He went crazy
And breathed fire and he ruined the party.

Kyron Lloyd White (7)
Ysgol Carreg Hirfaen, Cwmann

Sunny

My monster's name
Is Sunny,
I think he's
Very funny.

Charlie Scaife (8)
Ysgol Carreg Hirfaen, Cwmann

Young Writers Information

We hope you have enjoyed reading this book – and that you will continue to in the coming years.

If you're the parent or family member of an enthusiastic poet or story writer, do visit our website **www.youngwriters.co.uk/subscribe** and sign up to receive news, competitions, writing challenges and tips, activities and much, much more! There's lots to keep budding writers motivated!

If you would like to order further copies of this book, or any of our other titles, then please give us a call or order via your online account.

Young Writers
Remus House
Coltsfoot Drive
Peterborough
PE2 9BF
(01733) 890066
info@youngwriters.co.uk

Join in the conversation!
Tips, news, giveaways and much more!

 YoungWritersUK  YoungWritersCW  youngwriterscw

Scan me to watch the **Monster Poetry Video**